A PICTURE *IS* WORTH A THOUSAND WORDS

A DEVELOPMENTALLY APPROPRIATE APPROACH TO EARLY LEARNING AND BEHAVIOR MANAGEMENT FOR TEACHERS AND PARENTS OF YOUNG CHILDREN

Seebaum, Matthew S.
 A Picture *Is* Worth a Thousand Words: A developmentally appropriate approach
to early learning and behavior management for teachers and parents of young children
Copyright © 1999 aha! Process, Inc. 166 pp.
 Bibliography pp. 161-163
 ISBN 0-9647437-6-0

1. Education   2. Sociology   3. Title

Matthew S. Seebaum

A Picture *is* Worth A Thousand Words

A Developmentally Appropriate Approach to Early Learning and Behavior Management for Teachers and Parents of Young Children

CONTENTS

Dedication   7

Acknowledgments   9

Introduction   11

Chapter One:
   What's in a Picture?   15

Chapter Two:
   What's the Label?   23

Chapter Three:
   What's the Plan?   31

Chapter Four:
   What's the Sequence?   59

Chapter Five:
   What's the Schedule?   73

Chapter Six:
   What Just Happened?   89

Chapter Seven:
   What's the Routine?   99

Chapter Eight:
   What's the Story?   115

Conclusion   153

Appendix   155

Bibliography   161

About the Author   165

DEDICATION

To my son, Tanner, whose battle against the ravages of a brain tumor has taught me more about the human spirit, strength, and uniqueness of being a child than I ever could have learned on my own. His innate ability to be cheerful and active even when in pain inspires me and validates my belief that all children are precious gifts.

ACKNOWLEDGMENTS

A very special thanks to the faculties at Martin and Ballenger Early Childhood Schools in Lubbock, Texas, for their inspiring dedication to young children, which led to the conception and creation of this book. Thanks also to the faculty members at Van Alstyne Elementary School for allowing me to serve as their principal and for continuing to inspire me to share my message. Our time together was short – but most meaningful and rewarding to me. Thanks also to the staff at Altura Elementary in Aurora, Colorado, for supporting and believing in me during a very difficult and challenging time in my life.

Individual thanks to:

Paula Jones, a true pioneer in early-childhood education, who validated and encouraged me to pursue my instincts regarding appropriate early-childhood education.

Beth Burkhalter, a diehard child advocate, who always helped me see the humorous side of young children and the adults who work with them.

Janice Dudley, who allowed me to learn from her many of the ideas and strategies mentioned in this book.

Karen Burk, whose infinite patience and ability to work effectively with young children nudged me to put my ideas into words.

Dr. Ruby Payne, whose brilliant work with poverty-affected children and families inspired me to write this book, thereby adding an early-childhood dimension to her research.

Anna Elmore of RFT Publishing Company, for her patience and expertise in formatting this book.

Dan Shenk, whose brilliance as an editor helped to make this book more reader-friendly.

Without the loving support of my wife, Stephanie, and my son, Tanner, this book would never have come to be. Their patience, encouragement, and inspiration brighten my life.

INTRODUCTION

This book arose from my naive experiences as a fledgling administrator in an early-childhood school. My name is Matthew S. Seebaum, and in 1995 I took a job as an Early Childhood Specialist with the Lubbock Independent School District in Lubbock, Texas. In this task I served as the building administrator for Martin Early Childhood School, as well as a resource to kindergarten teachers throughout the school district. Martin School was not only a new job assignment for me, it was a new program being opened by the school district. This meant that the entire staff was new to this school, which added another dimension to the job. Previous to this assignment, I had served as a teacher in a multi-age kindergarten/second-grade classroom, which gave me a developmental foundation and helped prepare me for the administrative position of working with young children and the teachers who serve them.

As an Early Childhood Specialist, working primarily with young children from poverty-affected families and teachers serving these children, I soon realized that there was a great need for effective, concrete communication strategies to use with children with limited language and experiential backgrounds. My first clue came during the first few weeks of the school year when I found myself overwhelmed with children needing disciplinary intervention. It seemed that teachers were constantly dragging or carrying screaming and kicking children to my office. Most of the time this undesirable behavior was the result of a power struggle between the teacher and student that had escalated to a tantrum when the teachers stood firm and the children did not get their way.

Initially, I dealt with this problem by sitting down and just talking to the children in my office about their misbehavior, then sent them on their way. This, of course, was seldom effective and did not have a lasting effect. As the days went by, I began to see a common theme among the repeat offenders. As I sat and spoke with these children, virtually all had the same blank look on their face. It was at this point that I figured it out; they weren't understanding a thing I was saying to them because I was speaking in terms of abstract concepts with which they were unfamiliar.

After the difficult first few weeks of school, I decided out of frustration to do something different. When the next child throwing a tantrum came to my office, I got out my drawing paper and markers and went to work. I used my limited artistic ability to draw pictures of the concepts I was trying to talk about. Much to my amazement, it worked! Using pictures along with my spoken words helped the children connect concrete meaning to the abstract concepts I was sharing with them.

Since that time I have become an elementary school principal and continue to be very interested in developing strategies for teachers and parents to use with young children that connect concrete meaning to abstract concepts. With the help of many of my colleagues, I have found and tested a great number of pictorial applications, both in the classroom and home environments, which attempt to bridge the gap between abstract and concrete concepts for young children. The application of these strategies affects children positively in academic, social, and behavioral settings. The ideas to be discussed in this book will present simple, effective, concrete, and easy-to-implement strategies for busy teachers and parents.

I never would have imagined that the strategies that I began using several years ago would have such positive implications in so many classrooms and schools. I have taken many opportunities and received many invitations to visit school districts, present at national conferences, and consult with educational service centers on the very ideas and strategies that will be shared in this book. I travel often (primarily in the state of Texas at the time of publication); the strategies in this book have been successfully implemented in more schools than I can count. School districts that have particularly begun the process of using the strategies put forth in this book include: Dallas Metro, Houston Metro, Amarillo, Corpus Christi Metro, and Lubbock. The material in this book has been shared at a number of conferences, both national (Jim Grant Leadership Institute, Dr. Ruby Payne's Train the Trainers Training, SDE Spring Regional Conference, and the SDE National Conference on Multiage and Looping) and regional (Texas Association of Administrators and Supervisors of Programs for Young Children, and the Early Childhood Summer Institute of Texas). I frequently receive e-mail from conference participants from many states who daily use the strategies in this book in their classroom. What seems to be most useful to seminar participants and readers of this book is the simplicity and ease of using the concepts, both in the classroom and home setting.

The material in this book links indirectly to the work of many early-childhood researchers, but it is primarily original in nature. This is not to say that all of these ideas are completely original; they are not. But in writing this book, I have found that most educational practitioners using these strategies or similar ones have done so out of discovery and experience, not from reading scholarly or professional publications. The referencing in this book is intentionally kept to a minimum for readability, but the following educational researchers and practitioners share the following views on abstract and concrete concepts, and on the notion of using pictures to make abstract concepts concrete for young children:

- "While preschoolers have developed a wealth of concepts, they still find abstract concepts like time, space, and age very difficult to use in organizing their experiences" (Bredekamp 1997).
- "Early childhood educators have evolved approaches that are very successful in promoting children's engagement in challenging and meaningful problems and enterprises, for instance, by encouraging them to plan and review their work and to represent what they know verbally, pictorially, and through other modes of media" (Copple, Sigel, & Saunders 1984; Edwards, Gandini, & Forman 1993; Forman 1994; Hohmann & Weikart 1995).
- "Young children want and need to express ideas and messages through many different expressive avenues and symbolic media. Young children form mental images, represent their ideas, and communicate with the world in a combination of ways" (Edwards & Springate 1995).
- "A ... characteristic of young children that affects their ability to resolve conflicts is their tendency to think concretely. We know that children of preschool age are unable to deal with abstractions: They learn best when information is concrete and specific" (Evans 1996).

The beginning phase of testing and implementing the material promoted in this book began on a very small scale. It started at two early-childhood schools in Lubbock, Texas, in 1995. The staffs of the original schools quickly realized the usefulness and practicality of using pictures with young children in the early-childhood classroom for setting expectations and behavior management. The testing of the materials and strategies in this book also found its way into the homes of many children. The success of the pictorial strategies at school for the purpose of behavior management soon were adopted and adapted for use in the home environment; parents frequently work collaboratively with school personnel to integrate consistent expectations between school and home.

aha! Process, Inc. • (800) 424-9484

At press time, the strategies in this book had been tested and used for five years in hundreds of classrooms and homes. The strategies referred to in this book have been used with children from all social and economic backgrounds, but the vast majority of the children who have benefited from this framework come from the poverty population. Most of the educators with whom I work directly are involved in urban and rural areas affected by poverty and are dealing with all of the difficult issues inherent in working with this population. The information in this book is credible and thoroughly tested – and has been proven effective in many schools throughout the United States. The opening quotes at the start of each chapter in this book are of great meaning to me and were chosen to weave a sense of the trials and tribulations that I, along with many other principals and early educators, experience daily. I feel that the quotes speak directly to the people in early education who give 100% effort each day. It is my hope that this book will be beneficial to all educators and parents who read it.

PURPOSE

There are many ways to deal with young children's learning and behavior, both at home and at school. Some techniques prove to be more worthy than others. As teachers and parents, we often grasp for ideas and strategies that offer a quick-fix solution. Unfortunately, almost all effective strategies require consistency and a time commitment, and there really are no quick fixes that work effectively for sustained periods of time. Most of the time it is the natural inclination of adult educators, parents, and authority figures to deal with learning and behavior by verbally and/or physically letting the child know that what they have done is wrong. This is a knee-jerk type reaction that almost all parents and school personnel use because it "comes natural." We often tend to deal with young children as if they were miniature adults. This type of instructional approach and discipline is ineffective for the young child because young children think concretely, and adults think abstractly and mistakenly expect young children to understand abstract adult concepts. This book will offer simple procedures and ideas for helping young children take control of their own learning and behavior with minimal assistance from the adults in their life.

For the purposes of this book, children 3 to 8 years of age will be referred to as young children. The ideas discussed in this book have been thoroughly tested and are supported by current research. Early-learning theory and brain research have informed the approach that using various forms of pictures in the school and home setting will help young children make appropriate choices and give them a sense of control over their own actions. The ideas and strategies discussed in this book are straightforward – and simple to understand and implement. This book is written with the busy teacher/parent in mind and is intended to be a quick read and resource. Also, for the purposes of this book, developmental learning theories and research will be discussed only briefly, and the content will primarily be that of practical application of the use of various forms of pictures to help young children manage their learning and behavior.

HISTORY

Traditionally, educators in elementary schools throughout American history have focused primarily on learning the basics and have given very little thought or effort to teaching children such social skills as manners and sharing. Some educators feel that all social skills should be taught at home and that children should come to school socially intact and ready to learn academic concepts. Realistically, schools, families, teachers, and children have changed a great deal in the past 30 years and now, more than ever, children are coming to school with limited social skills. It is important for schools and parents to realize that social learning is just as essential for young children as academic learning. The early-childhood classroom (preschool and kindergarten) in the last 20 years has seen a major philosophical shift from teachers setting up social learning environments to teachers pushing academics on young learners who are not developmentally ready to grasp many of the abstract concepts put forth. The hard push for academics in early-childhood classrooms has been the direct result of standardized testing trickling down through the grade levels. In reality, most kindergarten classes in the United States are just watered-down first-grade classes, and the other grades tend to follow suit. Unfortunately, for the child with limited ability in language, social skills, and abstract thinking, school becomes a place of failure, which eventually leads to acting out due to frustration with the constraints of the overly academic classroom.

Indeed, it is very difficult for most young children to master academic concepts in school if they have not acquired social skills and abstract-thinking ability. Lack of social skills in the young child usually has two results in the classroom setting: The socially inept child will either withdraw or act out due to frustration with his/her environment. Many young children with minimal social skills and limited abstract-thinking ability are often inappropriately labeled and placed in Special Education. There must be a place in early-childhood education for the instruction of social skills, along with academics, in a concrete, developmentally appropriate manner.

The title of this book, *A Picture* Is *Worth a Thousand Words,* says it all regarding the content to be further discussed. The book lays out practical strategies to use with young children. The ideas discussed herein are useful for children from all social, ethnic, and economic backgrounds, but the material is particularly intended for use by educators who work with, and parents of, children from poverty. Finally, this book should be helpful to educators and parents involved with at-risk populations ages 3 to 8, Head Start, Title I, private day-care facilities, public day-care facilities, and other early-intervention programs.

aha! Process, Inc. • (800) 424-9484

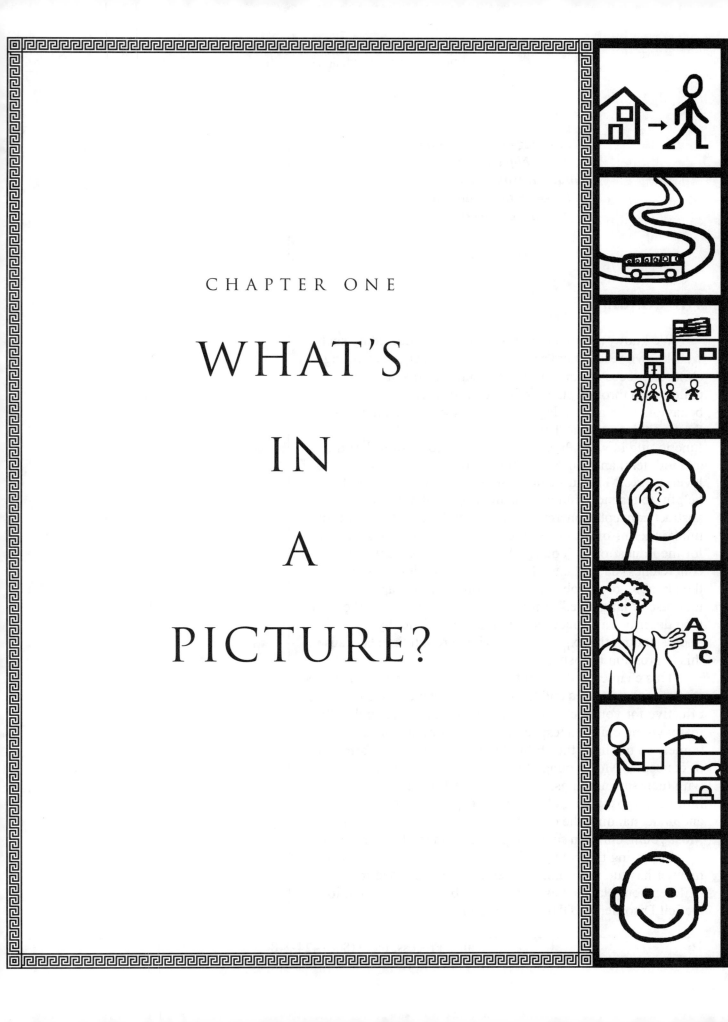

CHAPTER ONE

WHAT'S
IN
A
PICTURE?

*Knowledge arises neither
from objects nor the
child, but from interactions
between the child and
those objects.*

-Jean Piaget

THE CONCEPT

We know, through numerous studies conducted by such well-known researchers as Piaget and Kohlberg, that young children process information differently from adults. All children go through stages of development and exhibit certain behaviors with a high degree of consistency when they pass through these stages. This book will focus on children functioning in what Piaget calls the "Sensory-Motor" (infants and toddlers) and the "Concrete Operations" (early-elementary level) stages. The strategies discussed in this book will be helpful to teachers and parents in bridging the gap to make abstract concepts concrete for young children. Young children think in terms of concrete objects. The National Association for the Education of Young Children (NAEYC) defines concreteness as "[t]he tendency of young children to focus on the tangible, observable aspects of objects, as is apparent in their use of language." An example of this would be the child who describes a surface as rough, but has difficulty understanding the expression "having a rough time" because this expression is abstract.

This chapter will present an overview of the various types of pictorial strategies and techniques that have proven to be effective for young children. It is important to remember that many young children, especially those from language-limited homes, do not have the ability to process abstract information or concepts. Most young children are very literal in dealing with their surroundings. Since abstract-thinking abilities are limited in most young children, concepts such as time, space, and understanding the causes of human emotion are limited. Most young children function primarily in the here and now.

Educating the young child in the traditional public-school manner has run its course as is evident by more and more children being labeled as learning disabled, ADD (Attention Deficit Disorder), ADHD (Attention Deficit Hyperactivity

Disorder), and/or in need of Special Education. Essentially, what happens in public education to children who don't demonstrate abstract-thinking ability is that they fall through the cracks and have many behavioral problems because the traditional models of instruction don't meet their needs. These children are also much more likely to be placed in Special Education classes.

To better meet the needs of young children both behaviorally and academically, parents and educators can incorporate various types of pictures into the lives of their children or students. The use of pictures to help young children understand abstract concepts is not an entirely new idea, but it is an idea that has fallen far short of its enormous potential.

Using pictures with young children at home and at school is not a difficult or technical procedure; rather it is a useful and easy technique intended to bring about lasting changes in a child's learning and behavior. Pictures, as referred to in this book, can be photographs, hand-drawn pictures, computer-generated visuals, or manufactured line drawings. An important thing to remember about the techniques in this book is that the picture must fit the individual needs of the child. This book will guide the reader through the process of selecting appropriate pictorial measures to help young children understand concepts and expectations.

It is of vital importance to remember that young children must have a sense of control of their lives. For the child who lives in an ever-changing and unpredictable environment, learning is difficult. Just like adults, young children need daily routines and predictable sequences in their lives. Young children, however, do not follow the same sequential thinking patterns as adults. Young children often become very engrossed in one activity and lose track of a pattern of events. An example of this is the child who becomes upset when he/she has to change from one activity to another in school. When this happens, a power struggle often erupts in which an adult tries to direct a child to change activities. It's at this point that the use of pictures could help to illustrate predictable sequences to a child and alleviate the problem.

PICTURE THIS ...

Pictures of all types, shapes, and sizes can be used with young children to effectively manage their academic learning and social behavior. As suggested above, it's important to remember when using pictures with young children to make the picture fit the outcome. This means that the adult must take the responsibility of selecting for a child pictures that will help that child to make appropriate decisions. The type of pictures used with a child is just as important as the picture strategy used with that child.

Young children think concretely. Therefore adults must try to think like young children in order to understand their behaviors. The best way to get a child's perspective on the world is to listen to children. Listen to their observations of their environments. Listen to their language. Listen to the comparisons they make. Try to understand their frame of reference by observing them closely and, most importantly, try to understand that their behavior is usually a direct reaction to something in their environment.

Thinking concretely means that a child links tangible objects to prior and future learning. Concrete thinkers are very literal in their interpretations of their environment; clichés, puns, and euphemisms often are not interpreted by young children as they are by adults. Young children use their limited frames of reference to deal with new situations in their life. Most adults deal with young children by simply telling them orally what to do. For the young child with a small frame of reference and limited abstract-thinking ability, it is almost impossible to follow a task that is only given orally.

Adults, on the other hand, can think abstractly, and they have many frames of reference to which they can link new situations. Since adults are able to think through situations and scenarios quickly to make decisions, we tend to forget that young children usually don't have this ability. Thinking abstractly simply means that we, as adults, can envision situations and outcomes in our minds and act accordingly, based on what is in our memory. Another way to look at this is to realize that each of us as adults has a movie theater in our mind, and we're able to put together a film and play it in our mind almost instantaneously to make a decision. Although young children have the ability to imagine, they can't think abstractly to the degree that adults do.

Human minds think in images and pictures. In the book *In*

Their Own Way by Dr. Thomas Armstrong, an entire chapter is devoted to evaluating the effectiveness of teaching young children abstract concepts, such as the alphabet, without pictorial linkages. Dr. Armstrong refers to teaching the alphabet by saying:

> *Too many children enter the first grade classroom with high expectations, only to find a barren world of meaningless symbols on workbook pages, in basal readers, and on the blackboard ... most first graders see the alphabet with the right hemispheres of their brain, where spatial intelligence is generally processed. They see letters as pictures. An A is a couple of slanted lines with a horizontal line in the middle or a picture of a teepee or a mountain peak. In later grades, however, children begin to shift their perception of letters over to the auditory-linguistic area of the left hemisphere and learn to regard the letter A as an abstract symbol associated with a group of sounds (1987).*

When we encounter new information, we first search our long-term memory for comparisons to similar situations, objects, and events, then act according to what we have in our minds to compare the new situation to. Young children with limited experiences obviously do not have a lot of reference points, and when they are orally given instructions – or encounter unfamiliar, abstract concepts – they are unable to link these instructions and concepts to concrete experiences. It's at this point that the strategies to be discussed in this book are so critical. Linking meaning to words, behaviors, and expectations by using pictures is the primary focus of this book. This book will give the reader many suggestions on how to make abstract concepts concrete and meaningful for young children by linking meaning to pictures.

THE BASICS

There are many different ways to use pictures at school and at home to help children make better sense of their environment. The following brief descriptions of picture strategies will serve as a preview to what will be discussed in depth in the forthcoming chapters:

PICTORIAL AND WORD LABELING

Pictorial labeling involves making home and school environments child-friendly by assigning pictures to objects and areas. This strategy is used in developmentally appropriate early-childhood classrooms as a supplement to young children's language learning and development. This strategy requires adults to take the time to assign meaning to objects with pictures. This strategy can make home and school routines easier for children, while bolstering their learning.

PICTURE PLANNING

Picture planning is a technique that finds its roots in the study and practice of working with autistic individuals. This is also a strategy that has proven to be very effective for young children. This strategy is effective for children who have difficulty following instructions and staying on task. Picture planning allows children to develop sequential thinking to make predictions for learning and behaviors. Picture planning integrates the use of photographs, hand-drawn pictures, and line drawings into the classroom and home routine. Picture plans can be constructed by adults for children, or collaboratively between adult and child. There are several types of picture plans, including: social planning, academic planning, large-group planning, individual planning, routine planning, spontaneous planning, and predictive planning.

PICTORIAL BEHAVIOR STRIPS

Pictorial behavior strips are used for young children who have difficulty controlling undesirable social behaviors. Behavior strips essentially involve a series of behaviors represented in a sequence that makes sense to the child for whom the strip has been designed. Behavior strips are constructed collaboratively between a child and adult. This technique involves the pictorial representation of both desirable and undesirable behaviors. There are several types of behavior strips, including vertical, horizontal, and consequence-linked.

aha! Process, Inc. • (800) 424-9484

Chapter One: What's in a Picture?
A Picture *Is* Worth a Thousand Words

21

PICTORIAL REINFORCEMENT SCHEDULES

Pictorial reinforcement schedules involve a time interval and a tangible or intangible reward. Desirable behaviors are shown in pictures. When a child exhibits the desirable behaviors for a specified length of time, the child is rewarded intrinsically or extrinsically, depending on the needs of the child and the adult working with that child. Reinforcement schedules can be used for both behavioral and academic purposes.

SPONTANEOUS SKETCHING

Spontaneous sketching involves addressing a problem using pictures immediately after the problem occurs. This technique allows adults to bring immediate attention to a child's inappropriate behavior. Spontaneous sketching is used primarily for misbehavior, but it does have academic implications. Spontaneous sketching can be used for individual behavior redirection, social problem-solving, conflict resolution, and academic redirection.

PICTORIAL ROUTINE SETTING

Pictorial routine setting is used to help children understand and follow consistent routines and predictable sequences. Routines take place in the social and academic realms and are important to the success of a child at school and at home. Pictorial routine setting is a practice that can be used individually or in a group setting.

SOCIAL BOOKS AND STORIES

Social books and social stories are other techniques that finds their roots in the field of working with autistic children. A social book is an actual, personalized book that children can use as a reference to redirect their behavior. Social books are constructed by an adult for the child or by an adult with the child, then shared with the child. A social story is a strategy that can be used with the metaphor-story technique, which will be discussed further in the chapters to come. Social books and stories are usually not open-ended and involve a process and an outcome.

aha! Process, Inc. • (800) 424-9484

CHAPTER TWO

WHAT'S

THE

LABEL?

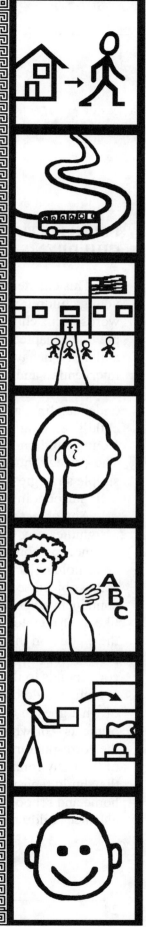

Strength of mind
is exercise,
not rest.

- Alexander Pope

USING PICTURES AND WORDS TO LABEL CHILDREN'S ENVIRONMENTS

This chapter will focus on the importance of labeling young children's objects and environments with pictures and words. This chapter will appear in a format different from the previous chapters because labeling is not just used to affect children's behavior, it can also be used as a proactive intervention and learning tool. Labeling should be used with all young children to help facilitate their concept understanding, as well as their vocabulary. Part of a young child's learning is experimenting with his/her environment. Young children learn a great deal from just exploring spaces. The strategy introduced in this chapter will explain some simple strategies to use with children to help them learn from their surroundings and assign meaning to their environment.

Any object in a classroom or home can be labeled to assign meaning to it and build a child's vocabulary. For instance, parents may choose to take pictures of some common household objects and attach the pictures of the objects to the actual objects, or they may decide to put pictures of objects on containers where an object belongs. To label actual objects like a refrigerator or oven, the parent would need only to tape the picture on the actual object and write the word under the picture. This helps a child see the printed word that corresponds to the object. An example of labeling a container at home would be to label the refrigerator drawers with pictures of what goes in them. A parent may take pictures of vegetables or meats – or whatever would be placed in the drawers – with the corresponding words. Young children become more aware of their environments when items and spaces are labeled and they build their vocabulary and organization skills. Some home and school examples of items that can be labeled to enhance children's awareness of words and organization are:

aha! Process, Inc. • (800) 424-9484

Home Labeling

* Kitchen items – stove, refrigerator, microwave, oven, sink, etc.
* Kitchen utensils – forks, knives, spoons, mixer, etc.
* Utility items – washer, dryer, freezer, etc.
* Tools – drills, saws, hammer, screwdriver, etc.
* Bathroom items – toilet, shower, sink, toothbrush, comb, etc.
* Storage areas and their contents – cabinets, shelves, etc.
* Areas – garage, living room, bathroom, kitchen, utility room, etc.

(See p. 29.)

School Labeling

* Storage areas and lockers – children's names and symbols on items
* Supply areas – crayon storage, glue, scissors, etc.
* Learning materials – clay, paper, folders, etc.
* Areas of classroom – library, quiet area, dramatic play, etc.
* Areas of school – rest rooms, cafeteria, gym, etc.
* Classroom centers – drawing, housekeeping, writing, sand and water, etc.

(See p. 30.)

Early-childhood educators have used labeling for many years and know the importance of this strategy to facilitate a well-organized learning environment. Labeling learning environments serves many purposes, including:

* Organization
* Vocabulary development
* Language development
* Print awareness
* Spatial relationships
* One-to-one correspondence
* Routine planning

Labels can be made by teachers or by children. The important thing to remember about labels is that the label must have meaning and link to a concrete object for children. Labeling environments is also useful for adults for organizational purposes, but children need to be the first priority when selecting appropriate labels for an environment. When labeling an environment, there are several guidelines to keep in mind:

1.   Labels need to be developmentally appropriate and have concrete meaning for children.
2.   Labels need to be introduced to children.
3.   Labels need to be attached to the objects they represent or be placed in the space for that object.

Guideline 1

Labels need to be developmentally appropriate and have concrete meaning for children

When labeling objects and spaces, an adult needs to keep in mind the developmental level of a child. Younger children need labels that make sense to them, as do older children. For younger children (ages 3 to 5), labels with words serve to build print and written-word awareness. Younger children also build their language and vocabulary by linking words with objects and spaces. Older children (ages 6 to 8) use labels for organization and word/print learning. The older child benefits greatly from seeing a word with a picture label to build his/her sight-word vocabulary. When selecting picture and word labels, please keep the following in mind:

*   Younger children (ages 3 to 5) respond more to the picture than the words, so picture choice is important.
*   Older children (ages 6 to 8) respond to words with the picture being used as a visual reference.
*   Photographs are a realistic way to label objects and spaces. Photographs are the preferred form of label to use with young children.
*   Computer-generated pictures work well with children who know and understand these types of pictures. In the

classroom environment, computer-generated labels work well.
* Adult hand-drawn pictures are not recommended unless the adult has artistic ability and the drawings have meaning to the child or children.
* Another source for labels is pictures cut from magazines or catalogues. Children can become involved in the labeling process using this form of pictures.
* Pictures need to be attached to paper backing so words can be written below the picture of the object.

Guideline 2

Labels need to be introduced to children

Once the labels have been prepared, they need to be introduced to the child/children. A good way to do this is to take children on a tour of the labels. This works well both at home and at school and simply involves the adult taking the children around the environment and showing them each label and saying the word for it. At a later time, the child will experience the label again and already know what the label is. Labeling an environment serves as a subtle learning and organizational tool.

Another way to introduce labels is to have children place prepared labels on the appropriate objects or areas. This offers a wonderful learning opportunity for children and an easy teaching opportunity for parents and teachers. Using this technique gives children ownership in the labels and allows them to link concrete meaning to the pictures and words on the labels.

Another labeling technique is to allow children to create their own labels and attach them to the objects and areas in their environment. Since many young children think in terms of concrete objects and experiences, using picture labels allows them to connect meaning to objects themselves. Creating their own labels – by either drawing them or finding pictures for labels from magazines and newspapers – allows children not only to connect concrete meaning through constructing labels, but attaching their labels to the objects they represent themselves.

Once children are introduced to labels in an environment, they will experience both pictorial representation of that object or space, as well as print and word awareness. Many children who are at the prereading stage of development enjoy choosing symbols to represent their names. This technique has been used in early-childhood classrooms for quite some time as a way to link symbolic representation to written names. Using this technique, teachers and parents use a symbol chosen by a child to label the child's belongings and environment.

Guideline 3

Labels need to be attached to the object they represent or be placed in the space for that object

This is a relatively self-explanatory process and simply involves attaching labels to objects and spaces they represent. Once labels have been constructed, they can be taped or stapled to the objects and areas they represent. As mentioned previously, teachers and parents can let children themselves attach labels to objects to connect concrete meaning to labels. Once labels have been attached to objects and areas, they serve as a learning tool for children to better understand their environment and improve their organizational skills.

SUMMARY

This chapter introduces the simple strategy of labeling environments and objects. Labeling is important for young children to make sense of their environments. Young children also learn organizational skills, expand print awareness, and bolster their vocabulary from a well-labeled environment. Labeling can be accomplished in several ways: Adults can prepare labels and label environments with pictures and words; children can attach adult-made labels to the objects and areas they represent; and children can construct and attach labels to objects.

aha! Process, Inc. • (800) 424-9484

Home Labeling

School Labeling

aha! Process, Inc. • (800) 424-9484

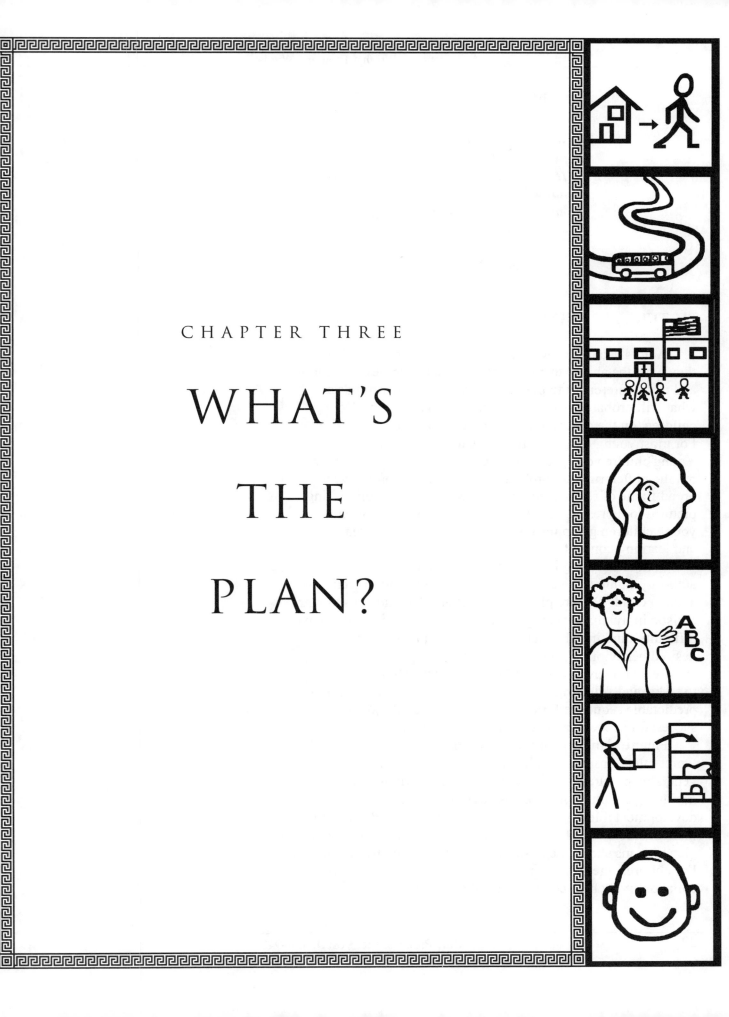

CHAPTER THREE

WHAT'S

THE

PLAN?

*The occurrence of a desire and
impulse is not the final end.
It is an occasion and a
demand for the formation of
a plan and method of
activity.*

- John Dewey

PICTURE PLANNING

Adults usually know what lies ahead in their lives because they have the ability to apply past knowledge to new situations and make inferences to play out scenarios in their minds about what will probably happen next in a given situation. Young children, on the other hand, usually have very little foresight. For most young children, life exists in the here and now. Young children can and do play out scenarios in their minds, but they often run into problems because they don't have a broad frame of reference to apply toward new stimuli. Using pictures to represent new and unfamiliar situations often helps young children grasp meaning and cope with new situations and learning concepts.

Picture planning is a process that requires an adult authority figure to be thoughtful, resourceful, and reflective about a child. Picture planning began as a technique used with autistic individuals, since people with this condition often have difficulty thinking abstractly and need frequent reminders of desired behaviors. Using picture plans is appropriate for young children who have difficulty following instructions, attending to tasks, and adjusting in various ways. Picture plans offer a predictable sequence for children to follow so they can be successful in social and academic environments.

Picture plans can take several forms. Picture plans can be represented through sketched pictures, photographs, computer-generated pictures, or manufactured line drawings. In designing a picture plan, one is advised to take the age and developmental level of the child the plan is being designed for into consideration. For children ages 3 to 5, as a general rule, picture plans should be designed and constructed by an adult. For children ages 6 to 8, picture plans can often be designed collaboratively between a child and an adult.

aha! Process, Inc. • (800) 424-9484

There are several types of picture plans, and each has its unique features and individual purposes. Picture plans can be used with large groups of children, or individually. It's important to remember the purpose behind this strategy when constructing a plan. The purpose behind all picture plans is to make an abstract task or behavioral expectation or group of tasks or behaviors concrete to a child. Picture plans serve this purpose well because they represent actions pictorially and serve as a point of reference for a child. The types of picture plans to be discussed in this chapter include: social plans, academic plans, large-group plans, routine plans, spontaneous plans, and predictive plans.

CONSTRUCTING A PICTURE PLAN

Once the need for a picture plan has been identified, the process of construction begins. There are several simple steps in designing a picture plan for a child. It is important for the adult designing the plan to remember that this process takes time initially to develop; however, the rewards from this process are usually well worth the investment. Nine steps are involved in designing and implementing all picture plans. Each step will be elaborated on in the pages to follow, and samples of all plans discussed will be provided.

DEVELOPING THE PLAN

The following nine steps are common to developing all picture plans:

1. Determine the area of difficulty the child is experiencing.
2. Consider the age and developmental level of the child.
3. Choose the appropriate type of picture plan to design.
4. Choose an appropriate sequence of events to represent pictorially.
5. Choose the type of pictures to use in the plan.
6. Gather the materials for the plan.
7. Construct the picture plan.
8. Assign meaning to the plan.
9. Implement the plan.

Step 1

Determine the area of difficulty the child is experiencing

This step is usually evident for the parent or teacher doing the preliminary work in designing a picture plan. Determining the undesirable behavior on which to focus the plan is usually very evident because it is what is obviously causing a child behavioral or learning problems. Behavioral examples of this would include: tantrums, saying "no" constantly, defiance, violent outbursts, uncontrollable anger, and difficulty with transitions. Academic and learning examples would be: lack of ability to pay attention, frustration, lack of ability to follow multi-step directions, lack of interest in learning, and inability to interpret abstract symbols like numbers and letters.

Step 2

Consider the age and developmental level of the child

This step is critical to designing an appropriate picture plan for a child. As adults, we naturally want to apply adult thinking patterns and expectations to young children. It's at this point when we must step back and try to think like a child. Try to look at a problem through the eyes of the child experiencing the difficulty. Often just trying to view a problem through the eyes of a child brings adults to a deeper understanding of the child and the issues surrounding them.

Age and developmental level are, at times, loosely correlated. We have been trained to assume that children will act a certain way when they are a certain age, and some generalizations can be made with validity. An example of this is the teacher or parent of a kindergartner who expects the child to have an interest in reading just because the child is 5 or 6 years old. These expectations have been ingrained into most adults and are products of public school systems' one-size-fits-all approach to curriculum and instruction. In reality, for children with limited abstract-thinking ability, age has little to do with readiness. Readiness usually comes from prior experiences, and many young children have been deprived of experiences, which makes them appear to not be functioning like their same-age peers.

aha! Process, Inc. • (800) 424-9484

When designing a picture plan, consider age first; make some generalizations about what the abilities of the child should be at his/her age, and begin to think of content for a plan that will have meaning to the child. Next, and most importantly, consider the developmental level of the child. A good way to compare developmental levels and readiness is to ask yourself the following questions about the child for whom you're designing a plan:

1. Does the child behave like his/her peers?
2. Does the child respond well to redirection and discipline?
3. Is the child able to read independently?
4. Approximately how long is the child's attention span?
5. How does the child react to frustration?
6. Does the child function cognitively at a higher or lower level than his/her peers?

Using these questions can help the person designing the picture plan to select a sequence of events that will have meaning to a child and help the child take control of his/her behavior and/or academic learning.

Step 3

Choose the appropriate type of picture plan to design

This process is difficult at first for the person designing a picture plan for a child. The best way to go about this process is to make sure you have accurately identified the problem the child is experiencing. Once you are confident you have identified the problem, you are ready to proceed into the next step, which is to choose the type of plan to design. The following is a list and description of each type of picture plan and recommendations as to which behaviors the plans work best for. These recommendations are not totally comprehensive and will not cover every possible scenario (as this is nearly impossible). The list and recommendations will, however, offer some practical strategies and solutions.

Social Plans

Social picture plans are designed for children who are having difficulties with social interactions. These plans are used primarily to help children manage their behavior through a sequence of pictures to serve as a reminder to the child of what is an appropriate choice to make and what is not. Social plans are useful for children experiencing problems with the following social interactions:

* Sharing
* Cooperating
* Following directions
* Staying on task
* Keeping hands and feet to themselves
* Listening
* Making independent choices
* Following through with tasks
* Controlling anger
* Controlling impulses
* Controlling physical actions resulting from anger

The social picture plan addresses a need for the child to correct an undesirable behavior. Of all picture plans, social planning is used most often. The social plan is usually individualized to a particular child, but in some instances an identical social plan is appropriate for more than one child or even a group of children. An example of a social picture plan made with line drawing is provided for a pictorial reference (see p. 51).

Academic Plans

Academic picture plans are used to help children make choices that will facilitate their academic learning. The academic plan helps a child to have a pictorial reference of learning expectations. Academic picture plans can be used for almost any learning difficulty that a child of normal intelligence is experiencing. Academic plans are not a remedial approach or a substitute for Special Education services. They can, however, be used for all types of children – from gifted to Special Education. Academic plans focus on the function of appropriate behaviors for learning. Often, when children see pictures of expectations for learning, they are able to use these pictures as guideposts to keep their learning behaviors in compliance with teacher expectations. Academic picture plans are used with children having the following problems:

* Lack of attentiveness
* Lack of organization
* Inability to focus
* Inability to stay on task
.* Difficulty following instructions

(See p. 51.)

Large-Group Plans

Large-group plans are picture plans used in a setting where many children are being served. The large-group plan helps to make directions and expectations concrete and clear to the young child in the school and day-care setting. These plans work very well for early-childhood teachers. A large-group plan can be used to represent to young children a sequence of events or expectations. A teacher would use a large-group plan for instructions or a reminder of previously specified instructions. A large-group plan can take several forms. These plans can be displayed in one place in a room for all children to refer to, or they can be photocopied and used individually by children. Large-group plans can be used for the following:

* Planning art activities
* Planning activities involving several types of materials
* Planning centers
* Showing step-by-step directions
* Showing social and behavioral expectations
* Displaying school and classroom routines

(See p. 52.)

Routine Plans

Routine planning allows an adult, or a child and adult, to create a pictorial plan that will help the child successfully accomplish a task. Young children need a sense of predictability in their lives. By establishing routines at home and at school, adults can help young children be successful. Predictable sequences are important in helping children maintain control over their actions and keep their emotions on an even keel. A routine plan can be used individually or with a group of children.

Using pictures to plan routines allows children to concretely understand expectations and see routines as valuable. Pictorially representing a routine requires an adult to analyze the steps the child must take in order to successfully complete a task. A simple example of this is a bedtime routine for a child. For the child who has difficulty going to sleep at night, a pictorial routine plan is an ideal tool to use. To design the plan, an adult should look at every aspect of the sequence, which may include: undressing, putting on pajamas, brushing teeth, story, then bedtime. For the routine plan to work, it must be followed consistently and referred to often. Routine planning is appropriate for the following problems and situations:

*   Moving about a classroom
*   Performing a multi-step task
*   Morning routines
*   Bedtime routines
*   Cleaning routines
*   Self-care habits
*   Schedules and timelines
*   "Transitioning" from one place to another

(See p. 52.)

Spontaneous Plans

The word spontaneous suggests that something happened on the spot or immediately, and this is exactly what happens with this type of picture planning. Spontaneous planning requires the adult in charge of the child to use materials on hand, which usually happen to be pencil and paper, and draw a picture plan for a child. The necessity for a spontaneous plan usually arises quickly, and the child needs to be dealt with immediately. The nice thing about spontaneous planning is that it is a quick process with immediate results. Spontaneous picture plans can be used for almost any type of behavior or social problem, including (discussed further in Chapter 5):

* Redirecting misbehavior
* Bringing clarity to unclear concepts
* Working with small groups of children
* Working with individual children

(See p. 53.)

Predictive Plans

Predictive planning is a strategy used by children to independently, or with the assistance of an adult, make plans for actions or solutions. Predictive planning requires children to predict what an outcome may be based on their knowledge, then design a plan to appropriately deal with that outcome. This is a high-level thought process, and younger children (ages 3 to 5) will probably require adult facilitation with this process. Predictive planning allows children to apply their knowledge and understanding of sequences and outcomes to a plan to predict what an outcome may be. This type of planning is very educational in that it causes children to think through abstract concepts and apply their concrete knowledge to generate predictions. Predictive plans can be used in the home and school setting to:

* Make plans to change behaviors.
* Prepare for transitions.
* Prepare for learning situations.
* Plan a multi-step task.

(See p. 53.)

Step 4

Choose an appropriate sequence of events to represent pictorially

This step challenges the adult facilitating a child to pinpoint exact events in a behavioral sequence. A series of behaviors exhibited by a child takes place in both academic and behavioral plans. The best way to determine a sequence of events to represent using pictures is to watch a child carefully as he/she is experiencing difficulty. An example of this would be the child who becomes frustrated easily when he/she is expected to share with other children. By watching this child to look for a sequence of events leading to a problem, an adult may see the child playing alone with a toy at the beginning of the sequence. Next, the child will be confronted by another child who wants the same toy. At this point, for the child who has difficulty sharing, a power struggle will erupt and the child will become angry and refuse to share. Eventually, the child who refuses to share will cry, strike out at the child wanting the toy, tattle, throw a tantrum, or pout. All of these behaviors are undesirable and can be remedied by a picture plan.

A picture plan for the child and situation mentioned above would show pictures for the following sequence:

1. The child playing alone happily with the toy
2. Another child entering the scene
3. Another child wanting the same toy
4. Both children struggling over the toy
5. The child refusing to give the toy to another child
6. The child crying

(See p. 54.)

This sequence shows the events leading up to the confrontation. The next step in this process is to show a solution to the sequence depicted in the previously described scene. This step requires the adult to decide with the child an alternative sequence of events to avoid this problem in the future. An example of a solution sequence to the sharing problem may be:

1. The child crying because of the sharing problem
2. The child thinking

3. The child going to the toy area with the toy and the other child
4. The child choosing a new toy to play with while letting the other child see the toy he/she was playing with previously
5. The child happily playing with the new toy he/she has chosen

(See p. 54.)

The process of choosing a sequence of events to represent pictorially is critical to the success of the picture plan because it allows the children to see things in a way that makes sense to them. This step in the process may take several attempts to get right because it's often hard to think in the same way that a young child does. It's important to remember that consistency pays off and, eventually, the plan will make sense to the child, and the child will be successful.

Step 5

Choose the type of pictures to use in the plan

This step requires the adult facilitating the child experiencing difficulty to determine which type of pictures a child will respond to best. In most cases, either a teacher or parent will be helping the child. For younger children ages 3 to 5, photographs or line drawings are usually most effective. For children 6 to 8 years old, hand-drawn pictures have shown to be effective, along with photographs and line drawings. The largest determining factor in selecting appropriate pictures is to know the child and his/her likes and dislikes.

A good way to determine what type of pictures a child may respond to is to watch the child when he/she is reading a book, watching TV, drawing, or playing. Some general rules of thumb for selecting appropriate pictures are as follows:

* If the child likes to watch TV and shows little interest in books with hand-drawn or painted illustrations, photographs will probably work best because they are realistic pictures.
* If the child likes to read books with hand-drawn or painted illustrations, hand-drawn or line drawn pictures will be effective.

* If the child enjoys drawing and creating with materials, hand-drawn pictures will be effective.
* If, when playing, children overdramatize or become very engrossed in their play, or if the children have a natural ability for art, this is a clue that the children are creatively motivated, and they should possibly draw their own pictures for their plan with the help of an adult.

The above-mentioned guidelines are only intended to be used as reference points and will not apply to all children in all situations. They are, however, useful when starting out with picture plans.

Step 6

Gather the materials for the plan

This step is self-explanatory and depends heavily on the decisions made in the previous steps. At this point in the process, you are ready to sit down and make the plan. Materials will vary depending on the type of plan you have chosen to construct. Listed below are basic supplies needed for the various types of plans:

1. Hand-drawn plans:

   * Pencils, markers, crayons
   * Paper
   * Glue stick, stapler, or paper clips
   * Laminating film (optional for durability)

2. Photograph plans:

   * Polaroid instant camera or 35 mm camera
   * Glue stick
   * Scissors
   * Paper or poster board for backing
   * Pencil, pen, or marker for labeling
   * Laminating film (optional for durability)

3. Computer-generated plans:

   * Prepared line drawings from Mayer-Johnson, Slater

Software, or other available picture communication symbols (see Appendix)
* Scissors
* Photocopier or computer with software and printer (see Appendix for software information)
* Glue stick
* Paper or poster board for backing
* Pencil, pen, or marker for labeling
* Laminating film (optional for durability)

Step 7

Construct the picture plan

This step is also fairly self-explanatory. It involves the process of actually assembling a picture plan. The illustration shows a completed plan, which should give a pictorial reference to the construction of the plan. Picture plans can take several formats, depending on the age, developmental level, and the needs of the child.

One rule of thumb that needs to be adhered to closely in constructing the plan: Children who are prereaders need to have the stages of their plan represented in order from the top of a page to the bottom since they are not yet familiar with left-to-right progression associated with reading the English language. Prereaders automatically look to the top of documents and then follow downward, which is a natural and comfortable progression for them. For children who are beginning to be proficient readers, a plan represented with left-to-right progression is appropriate.

Depending on the needs of the child for whom the plan is being designed, adults can complete the plan before sharing it with the child – or construct it with the child present and interact during this time. If the child in question has a very limited attention span, constructing the plan ahead of time is probably the best choice. For the child who is able to sit and pay attention for a short time (15-20 minutes), constructing the plan together is the best choice.

Most picture plans, whether hand-drawn, computer-generated, line-drawn, or photographed require transferring the sequence of the pictures onto paper of some sort. An example of this is the picture plan shown previously, which was designed for a 4-year-old. The construction of the plan involved cutting out the pictures and gluing them to the construction-paper backing. This plan was laminated so it would last longer for the child. The construction was a simple process that took little time to complete (see pp. 55-56).

Step 8

Assign meaning to the plan

This step is without doubt the most significant in the process. This is the step where the child connects meaning to the plan. The child assigns concrete meaning to the symbols of abstract concepts that will affect his/her behavior. The adult has a key role in this process, and effective communication with the child is of vital importance. In this step, the adult sits down with the child and communicates the plan to the child. There is some background to this process, and several strategies that must be shared before the plan can be effectively implemented. There are several proven techniques to use to ensure that the child connects meaning with the plan.

Language Registers

Language registers are the different ways in which we communicate verbally. An example would be the differences in our language from when we are at work as an educator compared with when we are at home with family and/or friends. There are five registers in every language as identified by Martin Joos in his research in 1967. Joos found that the five registers are characterized by various factors shown on the diagram on the following page.

REGISTER	EXPLANATION
Frozen	Language that is always the same. For example: Lord's Prayer, wedding vows, etc.
Formal	The standard sentence syntax and word choice of work and school. Has complete sentences and specific word choice.
Consultative	Formal register when used in conversation. Discourse pattern is not quite as direct as formal register.
Casual	Language between friends and is characterized by a 400- to 800-word vocabulary. Word choice is general and not specific. Conversation is dependent upon non-verbal assists. Sentence syntax is often incomplete.
Intimate	Language between lovers or twins. Language of sexual harassment.

(Sources: Martin Joos, 1967, and Ruby K. Payne, 1998)

In his research, Joos found that a person can drop down one register in a conversation, and it will be socially accepted. However, to drop two or more registers is considered to be socially offensive. When we communicate with children, this rule also applies. Dr. Ruby Payne (1998), who has conducted a great deal of research on the culture of poverty, found that children from poverty-affected families generally use the casual-language register and often don't have access to the formal-language register at home. This presents a problem for many children when they enter school because schools tend to use the formal register of language. Lack of understanding of language registers can lead children to unintentionally misbehave because they don't know the "rules" of school.

Formal language is part of life for anyone living in the United States. This is the language of careers. When children who have access only to the casual register of language become adults, they often find themselves having great difficulty functioning in society – especially the professional segment of society associated with employment. School is also difficult for children with limited formal-register language because instruction is delivered in this register, and everything from textbooks to standardized tests also is written in this register. Knowledge of language registers is important for the adult who is developing a pictorial plan with a child because:

1. Communication is necessary to convey concrete meaning and link actions to pictures.
2. A child's foremost communication style and language register is what should be used when discussing the plan with the child.
3. Using the appropriate language register gives concrete meaning to abstract concepts.

Metaphor Stories

Metaphor stories are another technique for sharing a picture plan with a young child. In the book *A Framework for Understanding Poverty* by Dr. Ruby Payne (1998), metaphor-story technique is used to deal with children who are reluctant for various reasons to communicate with adults. For this reason, the metaphor-story technique is also useful with picture planning. This process involves an adult using a non-judgmental and non-accusatory conversational tone with a child. Using this technique, the adult becomes a storyteller of sorts and lets the child interject the appropriate words when needed. This technique allows children to distance themselves from the problem for the purpose of confronting it later (while dealing with it indirectly in the present).

Metaphor stories keep a discussion "hypothetical" concurrently with getting to the root of a problem with a child. A metaphor story should be kept in the past tense so children can keep the linkage to their own difficulties "pretend." A metaphor story can follow any story structure a child is familiar with. Any language register can be used with a metaphor story, depending on which register is appropriate for the child in need of the plan. A few examples of how to begin a metaphor story are "Once upon a time," "I know a little boy/girl," "I am going to tell you a story about a boy ..." and "I need your help with telling a story." A metaphor story would also end with a solution and on a positive note.

Using Language Registers and Metaphor Stories to Assign Meaning to Picture Plans

The following example is an illustration and dialogue between a kindergarten teacher and a student from a language-limited, poverty background. The teacher is implementing a picture plan with the child, using primarily the formal register of language, but adding some references to casual register to emphasize certain points. The teacher is using the metaphor-story technique. The child's name is Reggie, and he is having difficulty controlling his impulses in class during large-group activities and center time:

T: Reggie, I want to tell you a story, but I need your help. Do you think you can help me?

R: Yep. What's this?

T: These are pictures of you that I want to talk to you about. Now Reggie, once upon a time there was a little boy who was in kindergarten, and he went to this school. What should we name this boy?

R: Reggie. Name him Reggie, like me.

T: OK, we'll name him Reggie. Now Reggie, once upon a time there was a boy named Reggie (show picture of Reggie) who went to kindergarten at this school. Reggie liked to draw and play in the gym. Sometimes Reggie didn't follow the rules in his class. What kinds of things do you think Reggie did when he didn't follow the rules?

R: Running around, yelling, saying no.

T: That's right, Reggie, those are some of the things that this boy did. Here are some pictures of Reggie doing some other things that get him into trouble. Do you see this picture of Reggie running away from the teacher?

R: He's running fast, like the cops gonna get him.

T: That's right. Why are the cops going to get him?

R: Because he been bad and fighting with guns.

T: Well, he is running fast, but do you think this is something we can do at school?

R: No, only out there (pointing to playground).

T: That's right, Reggie. Look at the next picture. It shows a boy lying down and crying and kicking on the floor. What do you think happened to this boy?

R: He got mad.

T: Why did he get mad?

R: Somebody dissed him.

T: Who dissed him to make him mad?

R: His friends said he couldn't play with them.

T: Let's pretend that Reggie in this story is a really smart boy, just like you. What could Reggie do in class so he wouldn't get in trouble by yelling, running away from the teacher, saying no, and kicking and screaming?

R: He could be nice.

T: How could he be nice?

R: He could say he's sorry.

T: That's one thing he could do. What else could he do before he did something mean or bad?

R: He could sit and listen to the teacher.

T: Very good. He could sit and listen to the teacher, and he could do things before he makes a bad choice so he wouldn't get in trouble. Let's look at some pictures of the good things Reggie could do so he wouldn't get in trouble. The first picture shows Reggie sitting at circle time listening to his teacher. The next picture shows Reggie asking his teacher permission to get up and leave the group. Do you know what permission means?

R: No.

T: It means to ask before you do something. The next picture shows Reggie thinking. When Reggie thinks, he can use his brain before he does something that might get him in trouble or hurt someone. Now let's look at all the pictures that will help Reggie do well at school.

The dialogue goes on to have Reggie keep a picture plan in his locker that he will refer to when he needs to be redirected. The teacher makes the transition from the plan being for a hypothetical "Reggie" to the plan being designed for the Reggie in her class. Reggie uses this plan whenever he has behavioral difficulty, and the teacher frequently reminds him to go to his locker and get the plan (see p. 57).

Step 9

Implement the plan

This is the last step in the process and one that requires the adult designing the plan for the child to be consistent and diligent with the plan until the child is familiar enough with it to use it effectively and independently. There is no time limit

aha! Process, Inc. • (800) 424-9484

for implementation since every child is different developmentally, and the implementation is contingent upon occurrences of the behaviors needing to be changed.

There are some general rules to follow when implementing the plan to ensure its effectiveness for the child for whom it has been designed:

1. Remember, lasting behavior changes in humans constitute a learned process and will not happen overnight.
2. Consistency is the key. Initially, the adult will need to go through the picture plan every time the undesirable behavior has taken place with the child.
3. The adult needs to remind the child of the plan before the undesirable behavior occurs. It is important to watch for warning signs and go through the plan with the child before the child exhibits the behavior.
4. When the child begins to use the plan independently before the undesirable behavior occurs, the adult can function as a facilitator and encourager. In this role the adult may simply give such reminders as "go and look at your plan" or "you used your plan well today; thanks for making good choices."
5. The plan may need to be modified once it has been implemented, because behaviors change. Some behaviors may disappear while others may appear. Remember that this is an ongoing process, and adults must be flexible. We all know that young children can be very unpredictable at times.
6. The ultimate goal for picture plans is to build in a child an inner cognitive sense of appropriate behaviors, whether they be academic or discipline-related. The child should eventually progress, through consistency in approach, to a point where the picture plan is no longer needed since the mental processes of the child now include independent thinking to control behavior.

SUMMARY

This chapter has taken a comprehensive look at the use of picture-planning techniques to facilitate behavior management and academic learning for young children. This chapter is the basis for the chapters to come and has purposely included a foundation for the subsequent chapters. Picture planning is the cornerstone of the preliminary knowledge needed to better understand the concrete needs of young children. Picture planning is an effective technique to use at home or school, and the ideas discussed in this chapter will be further elaborated upon in the chapters to come.

aha! Process, Inc. • (800) 424-9484

Social Plan, Vertical Format

Academic Plan, Horizontal Format

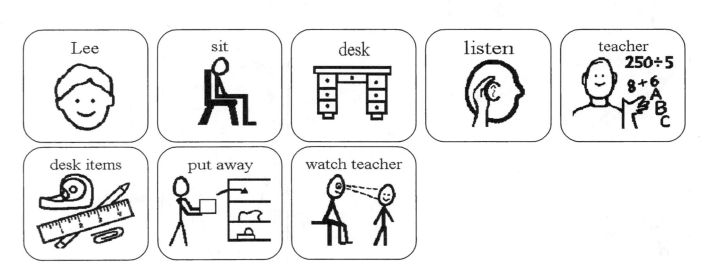

Large-Group Plan, Vertical Format

arts and crafts

fold

take a paper

dry

scissors

please be quiet

glue

book

crayon

cut and glue

Routine Plan, Vertical Format

Morning

Get dressed

Wake up

Eat breakfast

Get out of bed

Leave for school

Brush teeth

Take shower

Dry off

aha! Process, Inc. • (800) 424-9484

Spontaneous Plan, Vertical Format

Predictive Plan, Vertical Format

Hitting

No more hitting

Going to store

Renee' Crying

Put on coat

John mad

Get money

Solutions

Walk to store

John sorry

Buy items

Renee' happy

Walk home

Social Picture Plan, Step 4, Vertical Format

aha! Process, Inc. • (800) 424-9484

Predictive Plan, Step 7, Horizontal Format

Predictive Plan, Step 7, Horizontal Format

John	sit	get on bus
field trip	get off bus	sit
zoo	with teacher	ride bus
leave	go to zoo	school
school	look at animals	classroom
bus	eat lunch	

Using Language Registers and Metaphor Stories to Assign
Meaning to Picture Plans, Vertical Format

CHAPTER FOUR

WHAT'S

THE

SEQUENCE?

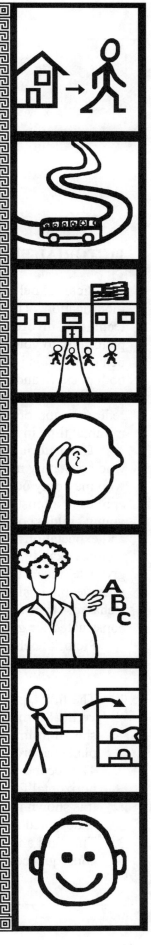

*Action may not always
bring happiness; but
there is no happiness
without action.*

- Benjamin Disraeli

PICTORIAL BEHAVIOR STRIPS

Pictorial behavior strips are used to supplement behavior modification. This technique, much like the picture-planning technique, involves representing a sequence of events pictorially to young children to help them manage their behavior. This is a simple procedure that involves representing both positive and negative behaviors. A pictorial behavior strip allows parents, teachers, counselors, and administrators to redirect inappropriate behavior quickly and effectively with minimal time investment.

The pictorial behavior strip should be used for children who constantly misbehave. It is not appropriate for children who may only occasionally have behavioral difficulties, as this applies to almost all children at some point or another. For the young child who has difficulty understanding abstract concepts and expectations, the pictorial behavior strip spells out in pictures exactly what are the behavioral expectations for a given setting. Pictorial behavior strips are physically manageable in size and convenient to use almost anywhere. Behavior strips are almost always child-specific and are rarely constructed for group use.

Pictorial behavior strips can be represented in three formats, which include the following:

1. The first type of pictorial behavior strip is called the vertical format. This simply means that the pictures are shown from a top-to-bottom progression. This type of plan is appropriate for prereading children.
2. The second type of pictorial behavior strip is in a horizontal format. This strip is identical to the first, except it is shown in a left-to-right, top-to-bottom progression and is designed for children who are able to read.
3. The third and last type of pictorial behavior strip is the consequence-linked strip, and it involves the display of

both desirable and undesirable behaviors, with the addition of pictorial consequences for inappropriate behavior.

DESIGNING THE PICTORIAL BEHAVIOR STRIP

When it is evident that a child is having constant behavior problems – such as tantrums, physically acting out, fighting, being disrespectful to adults, defiance, etc. – it is time to design a pictorial behavior strip for that child. Once it has been determined that the child can benefit from a pictorial behavior strip, there are several steps to follow to construct and implement the plan:

1. Determine the problem behavior.
2. Consider the age and developmental level of the child.
3. Choose the sequence of events to represent pictorially.
4. Choose the type of pictures to be used in the pictorial behavior strip.
5. Construct the pictorial behavior strip.
6. Assign meaning and implement the pictorial behavior strip, with or without consequences (depending on the child).

Step 1

Determine the problem behavior

This step is fairly self-explanatory, but important. In observing a child, an adult can pinpoint a problem behavior. A general rule of thumb to use with this type of plan is: If the behavior is constantly needing to be addressed with adult intervention, the child probably needs a pictorial behavior strip to be designed for him/her. When pinpointing the problem behavior, be sure to understand the nature of the behavior and what precipitates it.

For young children, lack of control of emotions is often linked directly to behavior problems. The adult must be able to understand the needs of the child exhibiting the undesirable behavior. For example, a child who is constantly getting into fights and arguments with classmates is probably dealing with a limited amount of patience, so the adult designing the strip needs to be aware of this when designing the strip so that the plan fits this need of the child.

Step 2

Consider the age and developmental level of the child

This step is important in that age and developmental level are the determining factors of appropriateness of the behavior strip. Age and developmental level are not always directly correlated, and some children don't fit the generalizations made regarding age. Many teachers and parents believe that when a child is a certain age, he/she should act a certain way. We know there are many exceptions to this rule, and we must look at the whole child and his/her actions when making a pictorial behavior strip.

The developmental level of a child is a much more reliable determining factor when designing a pictorial behavior strip. For instance, some first-graders are quite a bit delayed for many reasons, which leads to discipline problems for them. An example of this is the first-grader who is unable to sit at a desk for extended periods of time. There are many reasons for this, but the prevailing reason seen in schools today is that the first-grade curriculum is often focused so much on academic learning that insufficient attention is given to the social needs of young children. This obviously gives rise to discipline problems for teachers and behavioral problems for children.

When designing the pictorial behavior strip for the child with limited abstract-thinking ability, the adult needs to look at the actions of the child, not just the norms of age-level-appropriate behaviors. As an adult designing a behavior strip for a child, one should look at the child's actions that lead to the undesirable behaviors. This will help determine the design of a pictorial behavior strip that will have meaning and relevance to a child and subsequently improve his/her behavior.

Step 3

Choose the sequence of events to represent pictorially

This step involves the adult observing the child and his/her behaviors. It is important to observe all of the behaviors

aha! Process, Inc. • (800) 424-9484

leading up to a child misbehaving, as well as the behaviors that follow the event. When young children act out inappropriately at home or at school, they often don't remember the events leading up to the inappropriate behavior. Usually they don't even know they have misbehaved until they're reprimanded. This is why pictorial behavior strips are so useful in helping children see in a concrete way both the events that led up to a misbehavior and those that resulted from it.

The sequence of events leading up to misbehavior may not always be the same, and it's perfectly acceptable to generalize behaviors when designing a pictorial behavior strip. The most important part of this step is to pinpoint a sequence of events leading up to misbehavior. An example of this would be: A boy is very physical and often becomes violent with his peers during unstructured times (center time, outside play, physical education) when he doesn't get his way. The problem seems to stem primarily from a low frustration tolerance. The following sequence of events may take place before the violent outbursts:

1. A boy runs around out of control and bumps into other children, making them angry.
2. The children who are bumped into often push back and play rough too.
3. The boy does not follow directions when asked by an adult to not play rough.
4. The boy continues to play rough until he becomes involved in a situation that makes him angry enough to strike another boy and hurt him.
5. The violent boy becomes more upset when reprimanded and throws a tantrum, which involves profanity toward adults and other children.
6. After such incidents, the boy usually takes about an hour to cool off and resume normal activity.

Step 4

Choose the type of pictures to be used in the pictorial behavior strip

Much like picture plans, the types of pictures used have a significant impact on the effectiveness of the pictorial behavior strip. Usually, young children ages 3 to 5 respond well to photographs and line drawings. Older children 6 to 8 years of age respond well to hand-drawn pictures, as well as photographs and line drawings. It depends largely on the needs of the child as to which type of pictures should be used. Here are a few rules of thumb to remember when selecting pictures:

1. Know your resources. If you don't have access to computer software such as Mayer-Johnson's <u>Boardmaker</u> or Slater Software's <u>Picture It</u> (see Appendix), use photographs or hand-drawn pictures.
2. Know the child. If you know that the child responds well to one type of picture, use that type. Use no more than six pictures to represent a sequence.
3. Remember, photographs of each step in a sequence are often hard to get unless you set up a situation for a photo opportunity.
4. Remember, keep the process as simple as possible. Intricate drawings can often confuse young children and make their experience even more frustrating, as well as be time-consuming for the adult designing the pictorial behavior strip.

(See p. 70.)

Step 5

Construct the pictorial behavior strip

This step involves the actual process of putting the strip together. After pictures have been selected and collected, the pictorial behavior strip can be assembled (see illustrations for examples). The process is really very simple and only involves the following materials:

*   Construction paper or colored copy paper
*   Pictures
*   Scissors
*   Glue stick
*   Laminating film (optional for durability)

There has been a great deal of research conducted on the human brain in the past 20 years, and the research on human response to colors by Faber Birren is particularly applicable to pictorial behavior strips. Birren (1978) found in his research that different colors evoke varied responses in humans; he made recommendations and applications based on his research. For the purpose of constructing a pictorial behavior strip, knowledge of the following diagram is important:

COLOR	RESPONSE
Red	Good for creative thinking, short-term high energy
Green	Good for productivity, long-term energy
Yellow, orange, coral	Conducive to physical work, exercising, etc.; elicits positive moods
Blue	Slows pulse and lowers blood pressure; conducive to studying, deep thinking, concentration; accent with red for keener insights
Purple	Tranquilizing; good for appetite control
Pink	Restful, calming
Light colors	All-purpose; provide minimum disruption across all moods and mental activity
White	Disrupting, like snow-blindness; avoid

Knowledge of colors and their applications makes the construction phase of the pictorial behavior strip even more meaningful. The research on colors is valid and has been tested extensively. With some children, however, it will have very little effect, while with others it will make a difference. Another component of using colors in the construction of a pictorial behavior strip is to link colors with emotions for children who are prereaders. For example, the good or positive behavior side of the behavior strip may be green to signify "go" or "good," and it is also a color that stimulates productivity and long-term energy. On the other hand, the misbehavior side of the strip may be red to signify "stop" or "no," and it is also good for creative thinking and short-term energy.

To actually construct the plan, the person designing the plan needs to remember the previously mentioned guidelines. For either vertical (prereaders) or horizontal (readers) the procedure is essentially the same. The construction process includes the following steps (see illustrations for reference):

1. Using the color-application chart, choose a color to represent the positive (desired behaviors) side of the strip and choose another color for the negative (undesirable behaviors) side of the plan.

2. Cut the colored strips thick enough and long enough to show the progression of both the desirable behaviors and undesirable behaviors.

3. Attach the pictures (no more than six per side), in order of occurrence, to the behavior strip, either vertically or horizontally, depending on the reading ability of the child.

4. Attach the back of the positive side to the back of the negative side, making it a two-sided plan.

5. Add a consequence to the plan if it will benefit the child.

6. If you have access to a laminating machine, laminate the plan for durability.

Step 6

Assign meaning and implement the pictorial behavior strip, with or without consequences (depending on the child)

In this step, the adult will share the pictorial behavior strip with the child and then implement the strip. To share the strip with the child, the adult can use several strategies. Again, knowing the child and his/her likes and dislikes will determine the approach. For many children, just sitting down with them one-on-one will be enough. For others, the metaphor story approach discussed in Chapter 2 is a useful strategy. If using the metaphor story, remember that the plan must be "transitioned" to fit the child during the discourse. Below are a sample dialogue and pictorial behavior strip.

This pictorial behavior strip was designed for a girl named Kelly. Kelly is in the third grade and suffers from ADHD (Attention Deficit Hyperactivity Disorder). Kelly is not receiving medication for this condition and is having difficulty in class controlling both her impulses and physical composure. Kelly is an intelligent child and manages to do high-quality work when she is able to concentrate. Kelly's teacher has to constantly remind her to stay in her seat and remain on task. The teacher has designed a pictorial behavior strip for Kelly, which is shown. This is the dialogue the teacher had with Kelly when she introduced the strip to her.

T: Kelly, I want to talk with you about something today. You know I want you to be happy in my class, don't you?

K: Yes.

T: Well, there are some things that happen sometimes to

make my job hard and your learning hard. Do you know what I'm talking about?

K: Yes, I'm wild sometimes.

T: What do you do when you are wild?

K: I make noises and fall out of my chair and yell in class.

T: Kelly, why does this happen?

K: I don't know.

T: Can you think a little bit harder about this?

K: I forget that I can't do those things in school.

T: What can you do to stop doing these things?

K: I don't know.

T: I have something that I think can help you. What I have is some pictures to help remind you of how to make the right choices in class. Now Kelly, these pictures can be a secret between just you and me, or you can share it with your friends.

K: What are the pictures?

T: The pictures show you doing different things during your day at school. This picture strip has a happy side and a sad side. The happy side is green, and the sad side is red. The pictures on the green side show the things you can do to be happy and stay out of trouble at school. The red side shows the things that happen sometimes that get you into trouble. What side do you want to talk about first?

K: The happy side.

T: OK, these are the pictures of things you can do to stay happy at school. First, there is a picture of you smiling, which reminds you that this is the happy part of the plan. Next, there is a picture of you sitting at your desk. Next, there is a picture of you listening; see the ears? Next, there is a picture of you raising your hand and waiting to be called on. Next, there is a picture of Kelly standing next to her desk, which is OK if you need to do it – unless you can't handle it or unless it distracts other students. Last, there is a picture of you thinking, which is very important for you to do to control your behavior. Do those look like pictures of things you can do?

K: Yes, I can do it.

T: Now, let's look at the red side. This side shows Kelly with a sad face to remind you that the pictures are things that make you sad and get you into trouble. The first picture is of you yelling out in class. The next picture shows you on the floor and not at your desk. The next picture shows you not paying attention to the teacher. The next picture shows you bothering your friends so they can't learn. Do you agree that these pictures show the things that cause you to get into trouble in class?

K: Yes.

T: Now, we need to talk about consequences. Do you know what consequences are?

K: Yes, they are what happens when you get in trouble.

T: That's right, Kelly. Let's decide what will happen when you don't do the things that are on the green side of your plan and choose to do the things on the red side of the plan. Now, Kelly, I want to be fair with you, so I will give you three warnings per subject lesson to fix your behavior. But, if you get three warnings and still do the things on the red side, we need to decide what will happen. What do you think the consequence should be?

K: I could lose recess or have a time-out.

T: I think recess is important for you to participate in since you have lots of energy. Let's talk about time-out. Do you think you could quietly go to a place for time-out for three minutes and still listen to what is going on in class?

K: Yes.

T: OK, Kelly, we'll try this plan and see how it works. Thanks for working at this with me.

The dialogue continues to progress, and Kelly decides that she wants the pictorial behavior strip to be shared with her classmates and not kept a secret. Kelly agrees to keep the strip on her desk, and the teacher will subtly move the strip to the appropriate side during classroom instruction. Kelly knows that if the teacher turns the strip over to the red side that this will be her first warning and a reminder to look at the strip and decide which inappropriate behavior she is exhibiting and correct it. If Kelly corrects the behavior, the teacher will turn it back over to green, and this process will continue as long as needed. Kelly knows that each time the strip is turned over to red, it will be a warning.

This particular pictorial behavior strip with this child was very successful, and the child was able eventually to move the strip to a private place in her desk and make choices independently to correct her behavior. The teacher was amazed by the effectiveness of this strip, and her job became much easier as Kelly understood her plan.

The most important part of implementing a pictorial behavior strip is the consistency of reference to the strip. In the above-mentioned case, the teacher did a commendable job of making the child feel comfortable with the strip and giving her a choice about its implementation. This technique can be simple and effective when the steps are followed – and the adult takes the time to be consistent with its implementation (see p. 71).

SUMMARY

This chapter has taken an in-depth look at the use of pictorial behavior strips with young children. The steps described in this chapter are important for the successful implementation of a strip with a child. Children ages 3 to 8 have consistently responded well to this approach. The type of pictorial behavior strip used with a child is important. A young child must connect meaning to the strip for it to be effective, and the rules for the three types of strips should be followed closely. Vertical strips should be used for prereaders. Horizontal strips should be used for readers. Consequence-linked strips should be used for children who need this type of follow-through and consistency.

Pictorial Behavior Strip, Step 4, Vertical Format

Brittany	Brittany
happy	mad
sit	hit others
nice	yell
listen	bite others
share	mean

aha! Process, Inc. • (800) 424-9484

Pictorial Behavior Strip, Step 6, Horizontal Format

CHAPTER FIVE

WHAT'S

THE

SCHEDULE?

*We are beginning to see the end of
people relating to each other through
force, dictatorship, obedience, and
stereotypical categories. We are
beginning to relate through cooperation,
choice, empowering leadership, and
a real understanding of being
more fully human.*

- Virginia Satir

PICTORIAL REINFORCEMENT SCHEDULES

This chapter will introduce pictorial reinforcement schedules and the application of this strategy to the home and classroom environment. This technique involves using pictures with young children to make abstract behavior and learning expectations concrete for young children. This technique finds its roots in the behavior-modification techniques used by many child psychologists and counselors. The difference with the pictorial reinforcement schedule is that pictures are used to make behavioral expectations meaningful and concrete for young children. Pictorial reinforcement schedules involve a time interval and a tangible or intangible reward for appropriate behaviors.

There are two types of pictorial reinforcement schedules. The first type is the behavioral pictorial reinforcement schedule. The second type is the academic reinforcement schedule. The academic schedule is different from the behavioral schedule in that this type of schedule is used not only to modify behaviors, but also to modify habits for successful learning. The pictorial reinforcement schedules have the following characteristics:

BEHAVIORAL PICTURE REINFORCEMENT SCHEDULE

* Depicts positive behaviors in pictures
* Uses word labels for readers
* Involves a time interval
* Requires an adult to be consistent and interactive with a child

*   Involves either a tangible or intangible reward and intrinsic or extrinsic motivation

The academic reinforcement schedules have the following characteristics:

ACADEMIC PICTURE REINFORCEMENT SCHEDULE

*   Depicts positive academic behaviors and learning habits in pictures
*   Uses word labels for readers
*   Involves a time interval
*   Requires an adult to be consistent and interactive with a child
*   Involves either a tangible or intangible reward and intrinsic or extrinsic motivation
*   Does not have a consequence because it is linked only to positive learning behaviors

DESIGNING BEHAVIORAL AND ACADEMIC PICTORIAL REINFORCEMENT SCHEDULES

When it is evident that a child can benefit from a reinforcement schedule, an adult needs to follow a process of designing and implementing the schedule appropriately. Reinforcement schedules should be used only for children who are having chronic and persistent behavioral or academic problems.

For the behavior reinforcement schedule, an adult should look for problem behaviors exhibited by a child on a consistent basis. The child who is constantly being redirected and reprimanded for continual misconduct is a likely candidate for the behavior reinforcement schedule. A reinforcement schedule should be reserved primarily for children who have a very short attention span. This type of schedule serves as a frequent reminder to the child of expected behaviors. The goal of the reinforcement schedule is to "transition" a child from having to be frequently reminded of appropriate behaviors to a child who can intrinsically control his/her behavior. Children who are most likely to benefit from a behavior reinforcement schedule tend to exhibit the following behaviors:

* Impulsiveness
* ADD (Attention Deficit Disorder)
* ADHD (Attention Deficit Hyperactivity Disorder)
* Short attention span
* Easily influenced by peers
* Easily distracted
* Lack of focus
* Acting out physically

Children who are candidates for the academic reinforcement schedule exhibit behaviors consistent with poor study habits and low grades. Often low grades are the result of a child being unable to follow school and classroom expectations due to lack of abstract-thinking ability and inability to follow a consistent routine. Children who suffer from ADD and ADHD often benefit greatly from the academic reinforcement schedule. Children who exhibit the following characteristics will benefit from the academic picture reinforcement schedule:

* Inability to focus during classroom instruction
* ADD
* ADHD
* Poor motivation
* Poor study habits
* Difficulty seeing tasks through completion

In designing the pictorial reinforcement schedule, one should be aware of several steps that must be followed for effective implementation. Both behavioral and academic reinforcement schedules follow these steps in the construction and implementation process:

1. Determine the area of difficulty the child is experiencing.
2. Consider the age and developmental level of the child.
3. Choose the appropriate type of schedule to design.
4. Choose the type of pictures to use in the schedule.
5. Gather materials and construct the schedule.
6. Choose the type of reinforcement to use in the schedule.
7. Assign meaning and implement the schedule.

aha! Process, Inc. • (800) 424-9484

Step 1

Determine the area of difficulty the child is experiencing

This step requires the adult to observe the child for whom the schedule is being designed, then pinpoint the problem. With pictorial reinforcement schedules, both behavioral and academic uses apply. For the behavioral schedules, the adult needs to determine if the child is exhibiting an undesirable behavior continually. If this is the case, the adult needs to determine the degree to which the behavior is occurring and the impact it is having on the child's success at home or school. If the behavior is affecting the child to a high degree, the reinforcement schedule should be designed.

For the child experiencing academic difficulties, the schedule designed needs to address both the academic needs and the behavioral needs affecting the academic concerns. Since academic problems for young children are often linked to behavioral and social concerns and lack of developmental readiness, it is important to keep the behavioral dimension of the academic schedule in mind.

Step 2

Consider the age and developmental level of the child

As mentioned in the previous chapters, knowing the developmental level of a child is vitally important in selecting an appropriate reinforcement schedule. A child's age is a determining factor in the selection of an appropriate schedule, but developmental level is more important and more indicative of the child's actual level of understanding. Another consideration is the time interval of the reinforcement schedule. Younger children have a shorter attention span as a rule than older children, so the time-reinforcement intervals will differ, depending on the child's age and maturity. In general, the following guidelines should be followed regarding time increments for reinforcement of appropriate behaviors:

AGE	TIME INTERVAL
3 years	every 10-15 minutes
4 years	every 15-20 minutes
5 years	every 20-30 minutes
6 years	every 25-35 minutes
7 years	every 30-40 minutes
8 years	every 45-60 minutes

Step 3

Choose the appropriate type of schedule to design

This step requires the adult to analyze the needs of the
child and determine, by using the above-mentioned
information, which type of schedule is needed and an
appropriate interval of time for reinforcement. Since there are
only two types of reinforcement schedules, and the needs are
usually quite evident, it usually doesn't take long to render a
decision. If the child is constantly misbehaving in social
situations, then a behavior reinforcement schedule is needed. If
the child is having difficulty with academics – or concentration
in class or at home – then an academically oriented schedule is
needed.

Step 4

Choose the type of pictures to use in the schedule

This step is related to the steps mentioned in the previous
chapters in that the type of pictures used need to fit the needs of
the child the schedule is designed for. For the purposes of a
reinforcement schedule, pictures need to represent desired
actions which will be reinforced on a time interval appropriate
for the child. For picture selection for a pictorial reinforcement
schedule, the following guidelines should be used:

1. Know what the child responds to. If the child responds
    well to a certain type of picture, then use that form of
    representation.
2. As a rule of thumb, photographs work well with young
    children ages 3 to 5 because they are realistic and concrete.

aha! Process, Inc. • (800) 424-9484

3. Computer-generated pictures like Mayer-Johnson's Boardmaker and Slater Software's Picture It work well with 5-year-olds to 8-year-olds.
4. Hand-drawn pictures generally will work well for the reinforcement schedule for any child ages 3 to 8, if they are drawn with the child present.
5. Make sure the pictures show the desired behavior clearly and make sense to the child.

Step 5

Gather materials and construct the schedule

This is the process of actually putting the reinforcement schedule together. There are several rules to remember with this process, just as with all of the procedures in this book. The pictorial reinforcement schedule shows only desired behaviors. There is not a set sequence to the desired behaviors. The desired behaviors shown can vary in number. For some children, there may be only one desired behavior to attain. For others, there may be several behaviors that are related to one another and need to be represented in pictures.

Necessary materials for constructing the pictorial reinforcement schedule include the following:

*   Pictures of desired behavior(s)
*   Construction paper, poster board, or copy paper for backing
*   Scissors
*   Glue stick
*   Laminating film for protection (optional)

To construct the schedule, the pictures need to be attached with the glue stick to the construction-paper or copy-paper backing. Remember, the pictures don't need to be in a sequential order. Laminating the reinforcement schedule makes it more durable (see illustrations for sample of a reinforcement schedule).

To have a good day at school, I need to: Listen to my teacher, stay in my seat, be nice to my friends, do my work, keep my hands to myself.

Step 6

Choose the type of reinforcement to use in the schedule

This is an important step in the process because the reinforcement used with children is very individualized, and the success of the schedule hinges largely on appropriate reinforcement. Every pictorial reinforcement schedule must be effectively linked to a positive reinforcer/reward that has meaning for and impact on the child. The reinforcement schedule involves a time interval and a reward for the desired behaviors at the end of each time interval. For the reinforcement schedule, the reward/reinforcer must immediately follow the time period if the child has gone the length of time without displaying the undesirable behavior. The goal of the schedule is for the child to go a certain amount of time without displaying any undesirable behaviors, while at the same time displaying the desired behaviors shown on the pictorial reinforcement schedule. Eventually, through a consistent approach, a child's time interval should be extended until the reinforcement schedule can be done away with, and the child displays the desired behaviors independently – without the need for the pictures, rewards, or time intervals. This process takes time, commitment, and consistency, but the end result is well worth the investment.

The debate over rewards and reinforcers for young children is an issue that has been discussed among educators and child psychologists for many years. For the purpose of this book, a neutral stance will be taken on this issue, because each child has different needs and each parent and each teacher has a personal belief system and preferences of reinforcers. Basically, rewards and reinforcers are used to motivate children to perform appropriate and desired behaviors. Rewards and reinforcers fall into two categories: intrinsic and extrinsic. Intrinsic motivation refers to "a course of action set by oneself" (Howard 1994), and extrinsic motivation refers to "a course of action set by others" (Howard 1994). Intrinsic motivation for children in behavioral and academic realms involves the child wanting to perform satisfactorily because of an internal desire to do what is right. Many young children do not have the abstract-thinking ability to know the difference between right and wrong and therefore cannot be intrinsically motivated initially. Extrinsic motivation in the home and school setting takes the form of a child being rewarded with tangible objects for appropriate social and academic behaviors.

Ideally, all human beings should be satisfied with internal satisfaction of doing one's best, but realistically we live in a society where we must work for a living, and we are often judged by material possessions, which essentially makes us an extrinsically motivated species. Extrinsic motivators and rewards are usually tangible objects. Intrinsic motivators and rewards are usually intangible and are on the emotional level. The following are examples of intrinsic and extrinsic motivators and illustrate the application of each for young children in the classroom and home environment:

Building Intrinsic Motivation

* An encouraging word to a child
* A hug
* A pat on the back

* A "high five"
* Saying "Good work," "Keep trying," etc.
* Using positive language with children, even when they misbehave
* Anything on the emotional level to build positive self-esteem in a child
* Building a relationship of trust between the child and adult

Building Extrinsic Motivation

* Rewarding children with tangible objects
* Giving candy
* Giving stickers
* Giving rewards of any tangible form
* Making deals with children (e.g., you do this and I will give you this)

For young children, both intrinsic and extrinsic rewards and motivators can be appropriate. For the purposes of the pictorial reinforcement schedule, determining which type of reinforcement is used will depend largely on the child. Later in this chapter dialogical examples of both intrinsic and extrinsic motivation will be presented to illustrate the implementation of a pictorial reinforcement schedule.

Step 7

Assign meaning and implement the schedule

This is the final step in the process. There are several important components of the pictorial reinforcement schedules to keep in mind before examples are shown and discussed: (1) pictorial reinforcement schedules focus only on the positive dimension of a child's behaviors or desired behaviors; (2) children are not punished for not performing the desired behaviors within a time frame … they simply aren't rewarded or recognized; (3) this process is designed to help children gather the skills they need to be successful at home and/or school; and (4) this process, when done consistently, helps children build mental models, which will assist them for the rest of their school careers to know the difference between appropriate and inappropriate social and academic behaviors.

aha! Process, Inc. • (800) 424-9484

To assign meaning to a pictorial reinforcement schedule, the adult needs to discuss the process with the child since reinforcement schedules can be used for both behavioral and academic purposes. A sample dialogue will be shared for each type. Because some children respond better to extrinsic motivation than intrinsic, examples of each will be given.

The first pictorial reinforcement schedule has been designed for a boy named Joey. Joey is 6 years old, in first grade, and of normal intelligence, but he suffers from some emotional problems. Joey has a diagnosis of Oppositional Defiant Disorder (ODD) and language delay. Joey's parents are extremely concerned with his behavior at home and school. In the school setting, Joey is receiving counseling and speech therapy, and his teacher works very effectively with him. The parents need help at home and are willing to try almost anything. At home, Joey displays the following behaviors: tantrums, hiding from his parents, being verbally and physically cruel to his siblings, and urinating in inappropriate places. With the help of Joey's teacher, his parents have developed a pictorial reinforcement schedule. Joey's parents introduce it to him in the following conversation, using the metaphor-story technique:

P: Joey, I want to tell you a story today. It's about a little boy. What should we call the little boy?

J: I don't care.

P: Then let's call him Joey, just like you.

J: (no response)

P: Now Joey, once upon a time there was a boy named Joey. Joey was in first grade just like you. Joey went to school. Sometimes at school, Joey got into trouble, but other times he had a lot of fun. Joey really liked his teacher.

J: Hey, this story is about me!

P: It could be. Let me continue to tell you about Joey, and then we can decide who the story is about. Now at school Joey was trying hard and making himself and his teacher happy. But at home some things were happening that were getting Joey into trouble. Do you know what these things might be?

J: Crying and hiding.

P: Yes, Joey, those are some of the things that were happening. Do you know what else happened? Joey was sometimes mean to his brothers and sisters. And sometimes he went to the bathroom in the wrong places.

J: Like the closet.

P: Yes, Joey. That's right. Now to help Joey so he wouldn't get into trouble at home, his teacher helped his parents to make a special piece of paper for him. Do you want to see the paper?

J: Yes.

P: Joey, on this paper, there are pictures of four good choices you [making the transition to Joey being the person the plan is intended for] can make at home so you won't get into trouble. Every time you can go 30 minutes without doing one of these things, you will get something special.

J: What will I get?

P: We'll decide that together, but first, let me explain how this works. We will put these pictures on the refrigerator, and I will use this kitchen timer with the loud bell to set the time limit for every 30 minutes. If you can go for 30 minutes and do the things in the pictures, you will get something special. If you can't do the things in the pictures, you won't get the special reward, but the clock will start over every 30 minutes, so you have a lot of chances to get something special. Now, let's decide what you want your special reward to be. What is something special you would like to have.

J: Candy.

P: OK, what else?

J: Stickers.

P: Since candy is not a good thing to have before bedtime, let's start with stickers. We can go to the store today and you can pick out some stickers. Then we'll start using these pictures when we get home from the store.

Joey's entire family became involved with this plan, and it had very positive results. At first, as expected, Joey missed many opportunities to be rewarded because of inappropriate behaviors. But, after about two weeks, he began to understand the constant attention and focus by his family on his positive behaviors. Joey received a great deal of encouragement along with the extrinsic rewards (stickers) and, after two weeks, his time interval was increased to one hour. Over the period of six weeks, Joey's time interval had been extended to three hours. Eventually, through consistent positive reinforcement, Joey was able to cognitively internalize the appropriate behaviors expected of him at home and became independent enough to display the positive behaviors without the reinforcement. This is not to say, however, that his behavior was always perfect, but there was improvement. Joey felt successful and a sense of control over his actions (see p. 88).

The second pictorial reinforcement schedule is designed to help improve the academic habits of a second-grade child at school. The child is 7 years old, and her name is Lori. Lori is of normal intelligence and is able to produce quality work when she applies herself. Lori is a very loving child who needs a lot of encouragement. She has relatively low self-esteem. Her parents were divorced a year ago, and she is living with her mother who has to work two jobs to make ends meet. Her father has left town, and she hasn't seen him since he left. Lori daydreams a lot in class and becomes frustrated when she doesn't understand her work. Lori also doesn't work well in cooperative groups and tends to withdraw when she is put in this situation. Her teacher has designed the following pictorial reinforcement schedule for her. This is the introductory conversation:

T: Lori, I want to talk to you about some things that can help you learn in class. I know that you are sad sometimes and don't always understand your work. Do you know why this happens?

L: I don't know, but sometimes I don't remember what you said to do.

T: Well, today I want to share with you a way to help you remember the right things to do so you can learn in this class. What I have here are some pictures to remind you of the right things to do to help you learn. What things are happening in these pictures?

L: This is me crying because I am sad, but there is a line through it. This one is me with my friends. This picture is me watching you.

T: That's right, Lori. Some of these pictures show you doing things that will help you learn at school. The picture of you crying with a line through means that I don't want you to get frustrated and upset because you don't understand something. The picture of your friends is for you to remember that you can ask your friends for help if you need it. The picture of you watching me is to remind you to pay attention and listen so you will understand the directions. Do you think you can do this, Lori?

L: Yes.

T: We will try this for a while. The most special thing about these pictures is that you will get a reward that will make you feel better about yourself if you do these things for a period of time. Now, I know that you are really good at telling time, so we will give you something special every 45 minutes if you do the things on the list. If you don't do the things in the pictures, it doesn't mean that you are in trouble, it just means you will get another chance when the time starts over. Now you can choose for this to be a secret between just you and me, or you can tell your friends. Let's decide what your reward for doing these things should be. What would you like me to do for you if you do these things?

L: Spend time with me.

T: OK, how about this deal? If you make it 45 minutes and do all of the things on the picture chart, I will give you a hug because I know how much you like hugs, and I know you want me to be proud of you. Now, if you go three days without any problems, we will have lunch together on the third day – just you and me. Does that sound like a good deal?

L: Yes.

This pictorial behavior strip was designed to instill in Lori a sense of accomplishment and self-esteem while improving her academic study habits. The plan was successful, and Lori responded very well to the intrinsic motivation that came from the teacher, building her self-confidence. For Lori, the reinforcement schedule rapidly improved her classroom learning behaviors and made her feel successful about her accomplishments. Within one month, Lori's time intervals had been extended to half-day and, within six weeks, Lori no longer needed the reinforcement schedule. The teacher, however, continued to set up special one-on-one times with Lori (see p. 88).

SUMMARY

This chapter introduces pictorial reinforcement schedules. Reinforcement schedules can be used both for academic and behavioral purposes. It's important to remember that the reinforcement schedule involves a time interval and a tangible or intangible reward/motivator. The pictorial reinforcement

aha! Process, Inc. • (800) 424-9484

schedule focuses only on desired, positive behaviors and does not include a disciplinary or punitive component. Pictorial reinforcement schedules work well for children who are easily distracted and for children who have difficulty following a sequence of events.

Pictorial Reinforcement Schedule, Step 7, Vertical Format

Pictorial Reinforcement Schedule, Step 7, Horizontal Format

aha! Process, Inc. • (800) 424-9484

CHAPTER SIX

WHAT

JUST

HAPPENED?

*Difficulties strengthen the
mind, as labor does
the body.*

- Seneca

SPONTANEOUS SKETCHING

Spontaneous sketching is a technique used primarily to provide immediate feedback to a child who needs to be redirected. Spontaneous sketching is used mostly for behavior applications, but occasionally, it is appropriate for academic needs. This technique can be used at home, school, or just about anywhere you have access to paper and pencil. Spontaneous sketching is the fastest and most immediate of all the picture-related techniques. Spontaneous sketching is used for: individual behavior redirection, social problem-solving, conflict resolution, and academic redirection.

Spontaneous sketching provides an excellent opportunity for an adult to sit down with a child or group of children and spend time linking concrete meaning to abstract concepts. Since many young children don't have the abstract-thinking ability necessary to make independent decisions to redirect their own behavior, spontaneous sketching allows children to see and hear expectations. In general, a spontaneously sketched plan should take 10 minutes or less from start to finish.

This technique is intended primarily for immediate intervention and feedback. It can be used with an individual child for a long-term plan, but for the most part lasting plans should be more carefully constructed – like the picture plans discussed in Chapter Two. The spontaneously sketched plan allows the adult to enjoy interaction with a child or children and is a highly interactive process on the language level. This is an especially useful technique for teachers to use in the classroom during center times or independent work times where children often have difficulty staying focused on tasks at hand. This is also an appropriate technique to use during unstructured play times such as recess, Physical Education classes, and field trips.

DESIGNING THE SPONTANEOUS SKETCHING PLAN

As was previously mentioned, this technique is quick and easy to use. The process of designing the spontaneous sketching plan is a short one with only a few steps. There are a few rules to remember when designing a plan for a child:

1. The plan should have a top-to-bottom progression for children who are prereaders.
2. For children who are readers, the plan should have a left-to-right, top-to-bottom progression.
3. Pictures should always be hand-drawn.
4. Pictures should be kept simple and labeled with words when appropriate.
5. Pictures should show emotions.
6. Pictures should be drawn with the child/children present, and an interactive conversational discourse should take place during the construction, explaining the events depicted in the pictures.

There are four simple steps in the spontaneous sketching plan that need to be followed to ensure the plan's effectiveness in stopping undesirable behaviors:

1. Have materials readily available.
2. Intervene subtly and with a purpose.
3. Pinpoint the problem.
4. Orally explain the spontaneous sketching plan to the child/children while drawing it.

Step 1

Have materials readily available

This is a simple and self-explanatory step in the process. Since spontaneous sketching needs to be immediate, the types of pictures used are hand-drawn. Hand-drawn pictures require very little in the way of materials, and personal preference is appropriate here. Usually, larger pieces of paper (8.5'' x 11'' or bigger) work better because they allow the adult more room to draw and label the plan. It's also important that the paper and drawing instruments be stored at a convenient place in the classroom or home since accessibility and immediate action are critical components of this process.

Step 2

Intervene subtly and with a purpose

Often when young children misbehave, they are doing so out of an impulse that hasn't been thought through. When groups of young children misbehave, it's frequently the result of the snowball effect where one child in the environment begins to misbehave, and others follow suit. When children are misbehaving, or emotionally agitated and angry or upset, it's important to enter the situation calmly and subtly. The adult who will do the spontaneous sketching with a child or children needs to de-escalate the situation and gain the child's trust to effectively work with that child or group of children.

Knowledge of appropriate communication techniques for young children is a very significant part of this process. For young children to listen and process what an adult says to them, they must first trust the adult. Adults who enter an emotionally charged situation with a child or children need to first make sure the children are physically safe. After confirming safety, the next steps are crucial. The word S.O.U.L. is used to remember the four steps to take when entering into an emotionally charged behavioral situation. This is a key process to remember when preparing to make a spontaneous sketching plan for a child or children:

* S is for Silence. When entering a situation, refrain from talking, and listen to the children to determine the problem.
* O is for Observation. Observe the child/children and try to determine what the root of the problem might be.
* U is for Understanding. Try to understand the child and his/her behavior and actions.
* L is for Listen. Listen deeply to what the child is telling you. Then make your judgments and construct your spontaneous sketching plan accordingly.

With children and adults, there are certain factors of human interactions that have to be in place before effective communication can occur. The High/Scope Foundation (1995) has conducted extensive research on adult-to-child interactions and, based on its research, has found that there are five "building blocks of human relationships," which must be present for successful communication to take place. These "building blocks" are as follows:

BUILDING BLOCK	EXPLANATION
Trust	The confident belief in oneself and others that allows a young child to venture forth into action, knowing that the people on whom he/she depends will provide needed support and encouragement.
Autonomy	The capacity for independence and exploration that prompts a child to make such statements as "I wonder what's around the corner" and "Let me do it."
Initiative	The capacity for children to begin and then follow through on a task – to take stock in a situation, make a decision, and act on what they have come to understand.
Empathy	The capacity that allows children to understand the feelings of others by relating them to feelings that they themselves have had.
Self-confidence	The capacity to believe in one's own ability to accomplish things and contribute positively to society.

With knowledge of the building blocks of human relationships, an adult can confidently and appropriately enter situations that require spontaneous sketching. This step is important to the long-term effectiveness of this strategy.

Step 3

Pinpoint the problem

After entering into a situation with a child or children and following the steps introduced in Step 2, the adult is ready to pinpoint exactly what the problem is for the child/children involved. The problem will be one of four types, which are appropriate for spontaneous sketching:

1. Individual behavior problem
2. Social interaction problem
3. Conflict resolution between/among two or more children
4. Academic redirection

Once the problem has been identified, the adult is ready to begin the process of drawing.

Step 4

Orally explain the spontaneous sketching plan to the child/children while drawing it

This is the step where the adult gets to draw the actual pictures for the child/children while discussing each picture orally with them. This step requires the adult to draw, label, and discuss each step of the plan while holding the attention of the child or group of children. For children who are not yet able to read, the sequence of pictures should be shown from top to bottom. For readers, the pictures should be shown in a left-to-right, top-to-bottom progression, and pictures should be labeled with words explaining the actions. The following is a sample situation of a need for a spontaneous sketching plan. A picture will be shown of a vertical plan and a horizontal labeled plan for the same situation.

The setting is a kindergarten class with 20 children, a teacher, and a teacher's aide. A situation had come about during center time where four boys are arguing over the fireman's hat in the dramatic-play area. The situation is brought to the teacher's attention when she hears one child yelling at another and the four boys yelling at once and physically struggling. When the teacher approaches the situation, she first makes sure that nobody has been injured. Next, she listens to the boys discuss what has just happened. After the teacher has gathered all of the necessary information, she sits down with the boys to draw a spontaneous sketching plan.

The teacher sits down with paper and markers. She begins by saying what she has just observed and the dialogue goes as follows:

T: When I walked over to the dramatic-play area, I saw something that made me afraid. I saw four boys yelling and fighting with each other. Let's draw what I saw. I saw John, LeRoy, Mike, and Matt pulling on the fire hat. I heard someone scream, and I saw some mad faces. Look at what I've drawn. Does this look like what happened?

S: (John) Yes, but he started it, and I had it first! (Mike) No you didn't!

T: Right now, I'm concerned with solving this problem. We have drawn what happened. Now I want each of you to think of some solutions we could draw so this doesn't happen again. What is something we could do to solve this problem?

S: (LeRoy) We could share. (Matt) We could go play somewhere else. (John) We could make a new plan. (Mike) We could each play with it for a minute.

T: OK, you have each given a solution. What I would like to do now is draw each of these solutions and put this piece of paper right here next to the dramatic-play center to remind you of your solutions to the problem.

The teacher completed drawing and talking with the boys and then let them go back to what they were doing without having them choose one of the four solutions – in order to see what they could do independently. Two of the boys seemed to lose interest and soon went to other areas of the room. The other two boys took turns playing with the hat and incorporated it into a pretend fire station. The spontaneous sketching stayed posted for the rest of the day. After school the teacher took it down and threw it away. The plan had served its purpose, defusing a possibly explosive situation (see p. 97).

SUMMARY

This chapter introduced a simple and effective way to assist children immediately with their behavioral problems. The technique of spontaneous sketching is immediate and helps children redirect their behavior quickly. Spontaneous sketching is used for: individual behavior redirection, social problem-solving, conflict resolution, and academic redirection. This technique can be used with a single child or a group of children. Due to the nature of the approach of using pictures with children to make abstract expectations concrete, only hand-drawn pictures can be used. The materials needed for this technique are minimal, and so is the time investment, but the results and gains are almost always positive and helpful to busy teachers and parents.

Spontaneous Sketching, Step 4, Vertical Format

Spontaneous Sketching, Step 4, Horizontal Format

CHAPTER SEVEN

WHAT'S

THE

ROUTINE?

*We are the meaning makers –
every one of us: Children, parents,
and teachers. To try to make sense,
to construct stories, and to share
them with others in speech and in
writing is an essential part of
being human.*

- Gordon Wells

PICTORIAL ROUTINE SETTING

In Chapter Two, pictorial routine setting is briefly introduced and discussed. In this chapter, we will take an in-depth look at the applications of pictorial routine setting. Virtually all of the current research data on early childhood education call for young children to have routines in their daily school and home lives. As has been stated throughout this book, predictable sequences and routines add stability to a child's life and make the unclear clear to them. For most young children, lack of a routine causes stress and uncertainty. For many young children, their home environment(s) simply do not provide a consistent routine for many reasons. At school, however, something can be done to instill in children a sense of predictability and routine.

Making the abstract concrete through pictures is a way to help children make meaning out of their environments. The High/Scope Foundation has conducted extensive early-childhood research for more than 30 years. The data compiled by this group have clearly determined the need for routines for children. In fact, one of the major components of this early-childhood educational approach is called the "Daily Routine." The daily-routine guidelines suggested by the High/Scope Foundation (1995) are as follows:

1. A variety of active learning periods provide children with a range of experiences and interactions. These active learning periods include the plan-do-review sequence; small-group time; outside time; transition times; and, if necessary, eating and resting times.
2. Active learning periods occur in a reasonable, predictable sequence that meets the particular needs of the setting.

3. Experiences take place in an appropriate physical setting.
4. Each period involves children in active learning experiences in a supportive climate.
5. The daily routine provides a range of learning experiences.
6. The daily routine flows smoothly from one interesting experience to the next.

Children involved in High/Scope schools and learning environments are immersed in a rich learning atmosphere at school. The High/Scope approach is also unique in that parents' input in the educational process is highly regarded, and teachers and parents communicate frequently. This helps the home-school transitions to be smooth, enabling parents and teachers function as partners to educate children.

In the non-High/Scope school setting, the benefits of predictable sequences and pictorial routine setting can also be achieved. For both parents and teachers, a basic knowledge of the needs of young children and the appropriate use of pictures can be of great help at home and school. Adult expectations of children also need to be within attainable limits. Young children have a natural sense to play and learn a great deal through doing so. Play is an important component of their daily routine, and any routine designed through pictures for a child should include a time for the child to be able to release both creative and physical energy through play.

DESIGNING THE PICTORIAL ROUTINE

The process of designing a pictorial routine for a child is an important step in making children understand their complex world. Young children who have difficulty thinking abstractly find it very hard to understand the concept of formal time measurement. For young children who cannot tell and understand time, school experiences can often be frustrating. Young children often measure time internally as the passing of events. For example, a child in school may know that after the event of recess, the class goes to lunch – or after story time, school is dismissed, etc. When children measure the passage of time through this method, which is very common, a set schedule and routine are essential. Often children who misbehave at home or at school do so out of frustration with a change in the environment. A good example of this is the child who has been at home with his/her parents most of the time before entering preschool or kindergarten. When this child enters preschool or kindergarten, he/she experiences problems because of a lack of social experiences and a drastic change in routine and environment.

Pictorial routine setting can be used at home or at school for both behavioral or academic reasons. It can be used with individual children or groups of children. Frequently, academic skills cannot be gained for a child until that child is comfortable, secure, and understands his/her environment and daily routine. For some parents and teachers, following routines consistently is difficult for many reasons, including: busy personal schedules, limited time, overcommitment to personal and professional activities, lack of organization, etc. Some young children can handle this type of environment by developing coping strategies, but most cannot. In schools where educators have worked hard to see that children follow predictable schedules and sequences every day, there has been a decline in discipline problems.

To make abstract routines and expectations concrete and meaningful for young children, pictorial routines may be used – for individual children or groups of children. There are many appropriate applications of pictorial routine setting. The most commonly used home and school applications include the following:

* Moving about a classroom
* Performing a multi-step task
* Morning routines
* Bedtime routines
* Clean-up routines
* Self-care routines
* Following a timeline
* "Transitioning" from one event to another

When preparing to construct a pictorial routine, an adult needs to remember to follow certain steps to ensure the successful implementation of the plan for a child. The process of designing a pictorial routine is similar to the previous strategies, but unique in several respects. The six steps for constructing the pictorial routine are as follows:

1. Determine the area of need
2. Consider the age and developmental level of the child or children

3. Choose the type of pictures to use
4. Choose an appropriate sequence of events to represent pictorially
5. Gather materials and construct the pictorial routine
6. Implement the routine

Step 1

Determine the area of need

With pictorial routine setting, the behaviors exhibited by a child or children in need of this strategy are not always linked to misbehavior and academic difficulty. Some children who are frustrated with lack of daily routines will withdraw and become passive. These are the children who are easy for teachers and parents to overlook because the behaviors they exhibit usually are not inappropriate or offensive. There are several telltale signs that signify the need for a pictorial routine; these indicators run the gamut of behaviors:

* A decline in academic performance
* Withdrawal and passivity
* Lack of self-control
* Overly emotional (cries easily)
* Frequently misbehaves in social settings
* Unable to sit still
* Frequently asks "When do we go home?" "When is lunch?" etc.
* Appears to be "lost" most of the time
* Frequently off-task
* Is a "follower"; does not take initiative
* Watches other children and their actions instead of the teacher/parent

This list is not comprehensive, but it does give insight into some of the behaviors that children who will benefit from a pictorial routine may exhibit.

Step 2

Consider the age and developmental level of the child or children

A child's age and developmental level are important considerations when beginning to construct a pictorial routine. Age and developmental level do not always coincide. For instance, a child in kindergarten may be 6 years old but function more like a 4-year-old and vice versa. It is important to take a child's actions more into consideration than his/her age when designing a pictorial routine. There are three general guidelines to take into account when constructing a pictorial routine:

1. Children who are prereaders will benefit most from a pictorial routine that is vertical (top-to-bottom) in orientation.
2. Children who are able to read will benefit most from a horizontal (left-to-right, top-to-bottom) pictorial routine labeled with words.
3. The number of pictures represented in a sequence will vary, depending on the developmental level of the child. Children with lower levels of development can handle only a limited number of steps in a command whereas children who are more developmentally advanced can make sense of more steps.

Step 3

Choose the type of pictures to use

Using pictorial routines allows a child to concretely process abstract concepts and expectations through pictures. As with the other strategies suggested in this book, the success of a pictorial routine will hinge largely on the types of pictures used. There are several guidelines to follow when selecting pictures:

1. Photographs work well for pictorial routines. It is often valuable to "stage" photographs for the pictorial routine to help the child learn expectations.

2. Computer-generated pictures (Boardmaker and Picture It) also work well if they're available. The Boardmaker and Picture It software formats the plan in a sequence; all that is required is printing out the pictures in sequence.
3. Hand-drawn pictures work with some children with pictorial routines, but it is difficult to link long-term expectations to these pictures. It does, however, depend largely on the child and his/her response to hand-drawn pictures as to whether this would be an appropriate selection.

Step 4

Choose an appropriate sequence of events to represent pictorially

This is a very important step in the process because it requires an adult to carefully analyze every aspect of a sequence. After such careful analysis, an adult needs to glean only the most important parts of the sequence to use in the pictorial routine. Since the pictorial routine is essential to a child's success either at home, school, or both, the selections for pictures need to make clear sense to the child.

A good way to determine the events to represent in pictures for a child is to simply think through in your mind what the steps are in a routine. If you cannot visualize in your mind the steps, then do what a child would do. In other words, walk in the child's shoes through the routine and take note of the key steps in the process. A simple example for the point of illustration would be a bedtime routine. This would include, but is not limited to:

1. Undressing
2. Putting on pajamas
3. Having a snack
4. Brushing teeth
5. Getting into bed
6. Hearing a story
7. Turning out the lights – bedtime

The steps are just a simple example of what the pictures might represent. The important thing to remember is that the pictures should serve as visual cues to move the child from one activity to the next (see p. 111).

Step 5

Gather materials and construct the pictorial routine

This step will depend largely on the developmental level and age of the child and the type of pictures used. The pictorial routine can be made from photographs, computer-generated visuals, or hand-drawn pictures. The appearance of the routine will differ depending on the pictures used. The materials needed are relatively simple for each type of picture used:

PHOTOGRAPH ROUTINES

* Pictures
* Backing material (construction paper, copy paper, or poster board)
* Glue stick or rubber cement
* Pencils or markers for labeling (if appropriate)
* Laminating (optional for durability)

COMPUTER-GENERATED ROUTINES

* Computer and printer
* Laminating (optional for durability)

HAND-DRAWN ROUTINES

* Drawing paper
* Pencils, pens, or markers
* Laminating (optional for durability)

When constructing the pictorial routine, remember that the sequence of events, regardless of which type of routine is constructed, is of utmost importance. The sequence allows children to see what comes next in a sequence, which gives them a sense of control over their actions. The pictorial routine must also be accessible to the child/children at all times as a

aha! Process, Inc. • (800) 424-9484

reference point when needed. The pictorial routine can be displayed in many places at home and at school. The routine can also be made small so the child/children are able to carry the routine with them for immediate reference.

Step 6

Implement the routine

The ultimate goal of the pictorial routine is to help the child/children become confident with their surroundings through a predictable, consistent routine. Once a child has become familiar with a routine, his/her confidence has been built, and the child will often become completely independent of the pictorial routine and perform the desired behaviors independently and without reference to the pictures.

The implementation of a pictorial routine is much like the implementation of the strategies in the previous chapters. It requires consistency on the part of the adult, and it may require the adult to physically go through every component of the routine with the child/children until they fully understand the expectations. In the classroom setting, there is sometimes the instance where an entire class could benefit from a routine displayed in pictures. The end result is a successful, independent child who is able to take charge of his/her own actions at school and home. When the pictorial routine is ready to share with a child/children, an adult needs to present the routine to the child on a one-on-one basis or a group basis, depending on the type of routine designed. For the purposes of illustration, a sample of an individual pictorial routine and a classroom routine will be displayed with the appropriate implementation dialogue.

The first example is an individual pictorial routine designed for a 5-year-old kindergarten girl who has never been separated from her mother for any length of time. Sue is in a half-day kindergarten program. As indicated, she has been sheltered for most of her life up to this point and has very limited social interactions with children her age. It is the second week of school, and Sue's teacher is seeing very little improvement in Sue's behavior. Sue is having extreme difficulty making the transition into the classroom in the morning. She cries, screams, and wants her mother. This is a difficult situation for her mother as well, because she feels guilty if she leaves Sue this way. Recently, the teacher has been asking the mother to leave because she seems to be making the problem worse. This is not a good situation for anyone, as Sue cries most of the day and clings to her teacher and wails, "When do I get to go home and see my mommy?" To help Sue understand the progression of her routine at school, the teacher has designed a pictorial routine, which is displayed. This is the dialogue the teacher has with Sue when implementing the routine:

T: Sue, I know you have been very sad at school, and I know you want to see your mommy. I want to help you with this problem so you can have fun and learn at school. Do you like school, Sue?

S: Yes, but I want my mommy at school.

T: I know you do, Sue, but you can be happy at school and know your mommy will be seeing you at the end of every day. Let me show you what I have made just for you. What I have here are some pictures that will help you get through your day. You will get to have pictures at home and at school. Are you ready to see the pictures?

S: Yes.

T: Let me show you the picture of you. Now what we will do is have pictures of every part of your day at school and a few pictures of you at home. First, this is a picture of you at home getting into the car with your mother to come to school. The next picture is you at school getting out of the car. The next picture shows you walking to the outside door of the school with your mother. The next picture shows you saying goodbye to your mother. Does this look like something you can do?

S: Yes, but where does my mommy go?

T: Your mother goes to work in an office during the day, but she often thinks of you. We will see another picture of your mother in a moment. Now, the next picture shows you coming into class to see your friends and getting to start the day. The next picture shows you coming to the circle with a smile on your face. The next picture shows you going to center time with your friends. Then the next picture shows you at recess. After recess we have snack time, and this is a picture of you having your snack. After snack we have story time and large-group time. Next, it's time to get ready to go home. And look at this next picture. Who is it?

S: It's my mommy.

T: That's right, Sue, it *is* your mommy, and every day she will come to get you after you have done all of the things in the pictures at school. Do you think this will help you?

S: Yes.

This pictorial routine helped Sue begin to be successful and enjoy school. Sue's teacher also had to work with Sue's mother to implement the pictorial routine. Sue posted the home pictures on her refrigerator. At school Sue kept the pictures on the side of the teacher's file cabinet. Sue referred to the pictures frequently at first, but after a few weeks, she began to go about the daily routine independently. Sue still occasionally has difficulty coming back to class after long weekends and holidays, but the teacher keeps the pictorial routine handy for these moments, and Sue usually can get back into the routine quickly (see p. 112).

The next example is a pictorial routine designed for an entire class. This routine is for a Head Start class having difficulty during transition times in the school. It is the beginning of the school year, and the teacher can't seem to keep the children from yelling and running in the halls whenever the class goes to recess, lunch, and PE class. The teacher has decided to put together a pictorial routine and share it with the entire class. The pictorial routine is displayed; this is the conversation the teacher has with the class:

T: Boys and girls, I have noticed that we have been having a hard time following the school rules when we go to lunch, PE, and recess. Now, we have to be quiet in the halls so other children can learn. It's what we call respect for other people. I want to help you with this problem, so I am going to use pictures to remind all of us what we need to do in the halls and when we need to do it. All of you know that we do a message board in the morning each day. We will also put some pictures on this board, and we will look at them every day to remind us of the right choices to make. Are you ready to see the pictures for our day at school?

S: Yes.

T: We will begin with the start of our day. The first picture is of us getting off the bus and coming into school. Notice that there is a quiet sign there to remind you to come into school quietly. The next picture is of us sitting in our morning circle in class. Then we do our planning time. This picture shows us in our centers. The next picture shows us reviewing. The next picture shows us getting ready to go to recess. Now remember, this is the special time where we really need to try hard to be quiet and control ourselves. The next picture shows us in line, and the picture after that shows us at recess. Does this look like a good plan so far?

S: Yes.

T: When we come in from recess, we also need to remember to be quiet and control our hands and feet, so the next picture shows this happening.

The pictorial routine went on to show in pictures the entire day at school. The teacher posted and discussed the routine daily until it became fixed in the minds of the children in the class. The teacher posted a morning and an afternoon routine, since each routine contained many steps. The routine is posted on the message board, which is a place where all children can refer to it when needed. At first, the routine did not seem to have much impact, but after the teacher made a point to consistently refer to it every day, the children began to improve their behavior (see p. 113).

SUMMARY

This chapter introduces the concept of pictorial routine planning. Young children need consistency in their lives to feel a sense of control over their actions. This strategy works well for individual students and entire classes because it gives children a pictorial, concrete frame of reference for expected behaviors. It also gives them the security of knowing what will come next in a sequence of events. Pictorial routines can be used at home or at school for children needing a consistent approach to managing the events in their daily life.

aha! Process, Inc. • (800) 424-9484

Pictorial Routine, Step 4, Vertical Format

get undressed

good night

put on pajamas

snack

brush teeth

get into bed

read a story

Pictorial Routine, Step 6, Vertical Format

Pictorial Routine, Step 6, Horizontal Format

CHAPTER EIGHT

WHAT'S

THE

STORY?

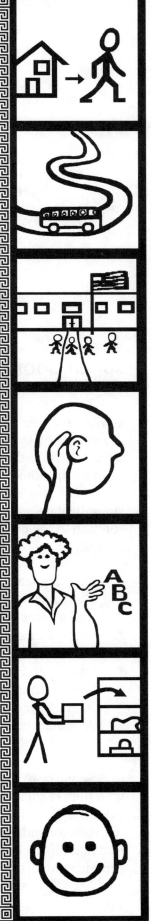

Children often show a
surprising sensitivity to the
personality of the teacher.
However difficult they are,
even under optimal conditions,
they can be guided and taught,
but only by those who give them
true understanding and genuine
affection, people who show
kindness towards them,
and, yes, humor.

- Anonymous, 1994

SOCIAL BOOKS AND STORIES

This chapter will explore the technique of social books and stories and their applications for working with young children. A social book is an actual book about an individual child, constructed for the child. A social story is the technique used to share the book with the child. Social books involve pictures, along with words for both prereaders and readers. A social story displays a positive beginning, a reference to a problem, a solution to the problem, and a positive ending. Using the strategy of social stories and books will help young children to:

* Communicate more successfully
* Gain meaning from what others tell them
* Make successful transitions
* Process meaning
* Follow directions
* Understand sequences of events
* Gain independence
* Interact socially with peers
* Associate concrete meaning with words, directions, and actions

Social books and stories are an effective strategy to use with both regular-education children and Special Education students. Social stories were originally developed to be used with autistic individuals, but recent research and application find that this technique can work with virtually any young child experiencing difficulty at home or school. This technique is so

aha! Process, Inc. • (800) 424-9484

successful because in large measure young children are egocentric individuals, and many of them truly believe that the world exists to serve them. This approach makes a personalized book and story just about the child. Children automatically assume ownership of the story because it is about them and their behaviors. The child then concretely assigns meaning to the book and, usually after a short period of time, the child exhibits the positive behaviors displayed in the social book.

DESIGNING A SOCIAL STORY AND BOOK

The process of actually sitting down and designing a social book for a child is an initially time-consuming process. It involves several steps, which will be discussed in this chapter. The need for a social book for a child will usually be evident by the behaviors displayed by the child. Social books can be designed for school or home use. This process becomes much easier after the first social book is designed and implemented. The steps in the process of designing a social book are as follows:

1. Target the difficult situation.
2. Consider the age and developmental level of the child.
3. Choose the type of pictures to use in the book.
4. Select the appropriate text to use.
5. Gather materials and construct the social book.
6. Assign meaning and implement the social book.

Step 1

Target the difficult situation

As mentioned at the beginning of this chapter, social books and stories serve children with varied needs, which can be both academic and/or behavioral. For teachers and parents, targeting a difficult situation is usually fairly simple since this is the behavior that is causing the child to act out inappropriately. Since social books and stories are individualized, the targeting of the difficult situation needs to fit as precisely as possible the behavior that the child is exhibiting. For instance, a child who acts violently toward his/her peers when put in a social situation needs a book that addresses this behavior directly. All factors contributing to this undesirable behavior need to be addressed in the book in both pictures and words.

Step 2

Consider the age and developmental level of the child

Much like the other strategies in this book, age and developmental level must be addressed. Since social books include both pictures and text, the appropriateness of the text and pictures is pivotal for the successful implementation of the book and story. When considering a social story, an adult needs to look at the actions of the child and his/her ability. The following questions serve as a guideline for determining the nature of the book, in accordance with the child's developmental level:

* Can the child read?
* Does the child enjoy being read to?
* How long is the child's attention span?
* Does the child respond well to written stories?
* Approximately how many words does the child have in his/her vocabulary?
* Does the child initiate social interaction with peers?
* Does the child become frustrated easily?

These guidelines will give the adult designing the book a frame of reference regarding the child and his/her actions. As a general rule, children who seem to be delayed in relation to their peers need a book with minimal text and more of a focus on pictorial representations of misbehavior.

Step 3

Choose the type of pictures to use in the book

The pictures selected need to make sense to the child. As in the previous chapters, pictures are an important part of this process because the child needs to connect concrete meaning to the pictures and internalize the appropriate actions displayed in

aha! Process, Inc. • (800) 424-9484

the pictures. For the purposes of social books, all three types of pictures discussed in the previous chapters can be used effectively in social books, depending on which type of pictures the child responds well to. When selecting pictures for a social book, keep the following in mind:

1. Photographs are the most realistic pictures to use, but photos of every action are often hard to obtain.
2. Pictures in social books may be mixed. A photograph of the child the book is designed for should always be used to link concrete meaning to the story.
3. Computer-generated pictures, such as Mayer-Johnson's Boardmaker and Slater Software's Picture It, work well for social books because they are convenient and usually specific.
4. Hand-drawn pictures also have been used very effectively; these pictures are best used when the adult is drawing the pictures with the child present.

Step 4

Select the appropriate text

This step requires an adult to develop the sequence of the story in the social book and select the appropriate words and types of sentences to be used. In this step, the adult must again consider the developmental level and age of the child. A book that contains too many words can confuse a child. On the other hand, a book that contains not enough text will only serve to frustrate some children. The adult constructing and designing the book knows the child and, based on the knowledge of the child, an appropriate amount of text can be used to fit the comprehension level of the child. Even prereaders can successfully "read" social books just by naming the pictures.

Before choosing the words to use in the social story, the adult needs to sit down with the child and find out what the child likes about school so the book can begin on a positive note and be appropriately linked to the child's interests. The adult also needs to talk to the child about possible solutions to the behavioral problems the child is experiencing. This information will be included in the book, both in pictures and words, and shared with the child in Step 6.

In a social story and book, certain types of sentences and

text should be used. For the story to follow a progression that will make sense to a child, the following sentences should be included:

* Descriptive sentence: tells where, who, what doing, and why. A good social story has one or two concise descriptive sentences (e.g., "My name is John, and I go to North Elementary School. At school I like to play outside and paint." Or: "Sometimes at school I make bad choices, and I hit my friends because I am mad").
* Perspective sentence: describes reactions and feelings. A good social story contains two or three perspective sentences (e.g., "When I hurt my friends, they cry").
* Directive sentence: individualized statements of desired responses … "I can, I will, I will try" (e.g., "I will try not to hurt other people when I get mad").

By using the aforementioned format, an adult can design the text of the story to follow a certain format so the child will become familiar with the structure of the story. Many children are already familiar with favorite fictional stories found in children's literature. Social stories mirror this story progression to some extent because they have an introduction, event or events that take place, and a solution. Below is a sample template of the text of a social story that will have coinciding pictures upon completion of the story:

My name is _____, and I go to _____
school. I am in _____ class. At school, I like to
_____ and _____. When I am at school,
sometimes I _____ and _____.
When this happens, I feel sad. To help me to stop
_____ and _____ I can _____.
I can also _____. This will make me happy.

This sample is often used when constructing a social book or story, and the appropriate words are filled in. Social stories can take many forms (this is just one example), but this illustrates the importance of choosing a text that a child can comprehend.

aha! Process, Inc. • (800) 424-9484

Step 5

Gather materials and construct the social book

Social books can come in all shapes and sizes. They can be very simple or complex and detailed. For the purposes of this book, we will focus only on the simple social book, since the end result is the same with each style. Materials needed to construct a social book are simple, everyday things found around the house or school. To construct the type of social books to be discussed in this chapter, you will need:

* The pictures that will be used
* Construction paper and/or 8.5" x 11" copy paper
* A stapler
* Rubber cement or a glue stick
* Pens or pencils to write the text
* Computer software program for pictures and text (optional)

To actually assemble the social book, you will need to decide on which type you are wanting to make. The simplest way to construct a book is to take three or four pieces of white copy paper and fold then down the middle and staple along the fold. This creates a book that is readily usable and durable. After folding and stapling, one needs only to glue the pictures and write the text. This book is small and compact. The other type of book involves using copy-paper sheets with a construction-paper cover and backing. If one wishes to use a computer program to create the text and pictures, this is the best type of book to use. For younger children ages 3 to 5 the bigger book is usually preferable because it's easier to manipulate when needed for reference. A picture sample of each book will be displayed in the next section.

Step 6

Assign meaning and implement the social book

This is the final and most important step in the process. This is the step where the adult works with the child to link the text and pictures of the social book to the actual actions of the child. In this important step, the adult sits down with the child and actually reads the story to the child while the child listens. The adult then reads the story again to the child, but this time the adult asks the child to name the pictures as the adult pauses. The book is read a third time by the child alone, with the assistance of the adult as needed.

The metaphor-story technique mentioned previously in this book is often a good strategy to use with children who are apprehensive about sitting down with an adult to share the story. In the metaphor story, a child can confront a problem in a safe manner by pretending, with the help of an adult, that the story is about someone else, just like the child in the story. When using this technique with a child to implement a social story, an adult needs to be sure to link the story to the child before ending the implementation dialogue.

For the points of illustration and application, four (two for one child) different social stories and books will be shared. Each will be prefaced with a brief introduction about the child and the situation, then followed by commentary regarding the success of the social story.

The first social story is about a boy named Kevin. Kevin is a kindergartner who is experiencing severe behavior problems at home and school. Kevin acts out violently when he becomes frustrated or doesn't get his way at home and school. Kevin has physically assaulted his mother, his teacher, and many of his classmates. Kevin is a strong child, and it usually takes more than one adult to restrain him when he becomes enraged. Kevin hits, kicks, spits, bites, and uses profanity when he has a rage. Often there are very few warning signs that Kevin may become angry, which makes it even more difficult for his teacher and parents. Kevin doesn't respond well to oral redirection and seems not to understand what the adults are telling him after he has a violent episode. Kevin is, however, easily soothed by close physical proximity (holding) by his teacher after he has had a rage. He enjoys being read a story after calming down. Kevin's teacher and principal have designed two social books for him. One will be to use at home with his mother; the other will be used at school. The following social stories and implementation dialogues are used for Kevin at home and school:

aha! Process, Inc. • (800) 424-9484

HOME IMPLEMENTATION DIALOGUE (between Kevin and his mother)

M: Kevin, I want you to share a story with me. The story is about you and me and our life at home. I have written it with the help of your teacher and principal to help you. Do you want to read it with me?

K: Yes.

M: This story has pictures and words, so you can read it by just using the pictures, or you can use the words. The story has a picture of you on the front of it and says Kevin's Home Book. Let's read it. "My name is Kevin, and I live in a blue house with my mom. At home, I like to play with my Nintendo and watch TV. I also like to play with my mom. Sometimes at home I get mad when my mom says no to me or won't let me do what I want to do. When this happens I get mad at her and I bite her and hit and kick her. This hurts my mom and makes her sad. This makes Kevin sad, too. Instead of hurting my mom when I get mad, I can go sit in my room and read a book until I cool off. I can also say, "I made a mistake" and tell my mom I'm sorry and give her a hug. Then I can be happy, and my mom can be happy, too!" Do you like your story, Kevin?

K: Yes, I do. May I read it now?

M: We'll read it together this time. Let's begin: "My name is ...

K: Kevin,

M: and I live in a ...

K: blue house with my mom.

M: At home, I like to play with my ...

K: Nintendo and watch TV.

M: I also like to ...

K: play with my mom.

M: Sometimes at home I get ...

K: mad

M: when my mom says ...

K: no

M: or won't let me do what I want to do. When this happens I get ...

K: mad

M: at her and I ...

K: bite her and hit and kick her.

M: This hurts my mom and makes her feel ...

K: sad.

M: This makes ...

K: Kevin sad, too.

M: Instead of hurting my mom when I get mad, I can ...

K: go sit in my room and read a book

M: until I ...

K: cool off.

M: I can also say,

K: "I made a mistake"

M: and tell my mom ...

K: I'm sorry and give her a hug.

M: Then I can be ...

K: happy,

M: and my mom can ...

K: be happy, too."

After the second interactive reading, Kevin read the story himself to his mother. Kevin's mother then told him that they would be reading the book every evening at home whether they needed it or not. She also told Kevin that any time he felt like he might get mad he needed to go and read the book to cool off. Kevin and his mother decided on a special place to keep the book in the house so it could be accessed easily. At first, the book had only minimal effects on Kevin when he became angry, but every time this happened, his mother gave him the book anyway. Kevin threw it a few times in fits of rage, but after several weeks he began to refer to it when he started to get mad. After about six weeks of consistently reading the book and using a similar book at school, Kevin began to show signs of the ability to control his anger himself. Eventually, after a total of three months, Kevin only needed the book occasionally. He did continue to get angry and occasionally threw a tantrum, but his violent treatment of his mother ceased, which was the primary goal of the social book and story.

Kevin's Home Book

My name is Kevin, and I live in a blue

house with my mom. At home, I like to

play with my Nintendo and watch TV. I

also like to play with my mom. Sometimes

at home I get mad when my mom says no to

me or won't let me do what I want to do.

When this happens I get mad at her and I

bite her and hit and kick her. This hurts my

mom and makes her feel sad. This makes

Kevin sad, too. Instead of hurting my mom

when I get mad, I can go sit in my room and

read a book until I cool off. I can also say,

"I made a mistake" and tell my mom I'm

sorry and give her a hug. Then I can be

happy, and my mom can be happy, too.

SCHOOL IMPLEMENTATION DIALOGUE (between Kevin and his teacher)

T: Kevin, I want you to share a story with me. This is like the story you and your mom read last night at home, only this one is to use at school. This means you will have two books of your very own to use. Did you like your home book?

K: Yes, it's going to help me.

T: I'm glad you are going to use it to help you. Now let's talk about the book we will use at school. This book is called Kevin's School Book, and you will get to keep it here at school. Why don't I read it to you? "My name is Kevin, and I go to North Elementary School. My teacher's name is Mrs. Smith. At school I like to play outside, eat lunch, and paint. Sometimes at school I get mad when my teacher tells me to stop doing something. I also get mad when I don't get to be the boss. When I get mad I cry, hit, kick, spit, and say bad words. When I do this I hurt my friends and my teacher. This makes them sad, and it makes me sad, too. So this won't happen, I can think before I hurt someone and go to a place to cool off. I can walk away, and I can look at my book and remember not to hurt people. When I feel better I can come back with my friends to learn and play. This will make me happy." Do you like your school story, Kevin?

K: Yes, it is like my home story.

T: Do you think it will help you?

K: Yes.

T: Now, I would like for us to read it together. Are you ready? "My name is …

K: Kevin,

T: and I go to …

K: North Elementary School.

T: My teacher's name is …

K: Mrs. Smith.

T: At school I like to …

K: play outside, eat lunch, and paint.

T: Sometimes at school I get …

K: mad

T: when my teacher tells me to …

K: stop doing something.

T: I also get mad when I don't get to be the …

K: boss.

aha! Process, Inc. • (800) 424-9484

T: When I get mad I …
K: cry, hit, kick, spit, and say bad words.
T: When I do this I …
K: hurt my friends
T: and my …
K: teacher.
T: This makes them …
K: sad,
T: and it makes me …
K: sad, too.
T: So this won't happen, I can …
K: think
T: before I …
K: hurt someone
T: and go to a place to …
K: cool off.
T: I can …
K: walk away,
T: and I can …
K: look at my book
T: and remember not to …
K: hurt people.
T: When I feel …
K: better
T: I can come back to my friends to …
K: learn and play.
T: This will make me …
K: happy."
T: Do you think you can read the story yourself this time, Kevin?
K: Yes.

Kevin read the story himself with his teacher and decided on a special place in the room to keep his book. Kevin chose to keep the book in his storage locker in the classroom; he and Mrs. Smith agreed that he could go to get the book any time he felt he needed it. Kevin also chose to share his book with some of his classmates during center time, and his friends were very receptive and supportive of the book. In fact, the first time Kevin became angry after the book was introduced, a boy in the class reminded him to go get his book, and he did. It took about four weeks for Kevin to use the book consistently, and the teacher reminded him of it often. After about four weeks of consistently using the book at home and at school, Kevin's behavior improved greatly. Within three months, Kevin phased the book out and internalized appropriate classroom behaviors. Of course, Kevin still needed occasional reminders, but his behavior did improve dramatically from when the book was first introduced to him.

aha! Process, Inc. • (800) 424-9484

Kevin's School Book

My name is Kevin, and I go to North

Elementary School. My teacher's name is

Mrs. Smith. At school I like to play

outside, eat lunch, and paint. Sometimes at

school I get mad when my teacher tells me

to stop doing something. I also get mad

when I don't get to be the boss. When I get

    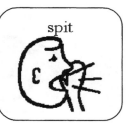

mad I cry, hit, kick, spit, and say bad

words. When I do this I hurt my friends

and my teac... ...em sad, and

it makes me sad, too. So this won't happen,

I can think before I hurt someone and go to

a place to cool off. I can walk away, and I

can look at my book and remember not to

hurt people. When I feel better I can come

back to my friends to learn and play. This

will make me happy.

The next scenario is about a girl named Lisa. Lisa is a second-grade student of normal intelligence, but she suffers from depression and low self-esteem. When Lisa is put in a frustrating situation, she cries and withdraws. Lisa is extremely disorganized, and this adds to her frustration. Lisa often becomes upset during times of independent work. Lisa has only one friend in the class. Her friend's name is Jamie; the teacher has incorporated Jamie into the social book she designed for Lisa. Lisa is a very quiet child and rarely will ask for help or initiate conversation. Because Lisa is falling behind academically, the teacher is spending time after school tutoring Lisa to help her keep pace with the rest of the class. The teacher uses the following dialogue and illustrations when sharing the social book with Lisa:

T: Lisa, I know that you have been sad at school, and I want to help you to feel better about yourself and your work. I have written a story about you, and I would like to share it with you. The story has pictures and words in it. Let me read the story to you. The book is called Lisa's Book. "My name is Lisa, and I go to Hoover Elementary School. I am in second grade, and my teacher's name is Mrs. Jones. At school I like to read books, draw pictures, and play outside. Sometimes at school I am sad. When I am sad I cry and put my head on my desk. When this happens I can't hear what the teacher is saying, and then I can't do my work. I get sad because I don't have my materials ready so I can learn and do my work. To help me with this, I can keep only the things I need on my desk. I can keep a pencil, an eraser, and my paper out on my desk. I can listen to the teacher, and when I don't understand something, I can ask the teacher or ask my friend, Jamie, to help me. This way I will not cry, and I can get my work done, and I can be happy." Does this story sound like it might help you, Lisa?

L: Yes.

T: (Skipping Step 2 – teacher reading with child) Since you are a second-grader, and I know you are a good reader, I want you to read the story to me, and I will help you if you need it. Are you ready?

L: Lisa's Book. "My name is Lisa, and I go to ..."

Since Lisa is a proficient reader and responds well to print, the teacher did not feel that it was necessary to go through Step 2. Lisa read the book twice to the teacher, after which the teacher asked Lisa where she wanted to keep the book. Lisa chose to keep it at her desk for quick reference. At first, the book had very little impact on Lisa, but the teacher was very diligent and kept referring Lisa to the book when she became frustrated. Lisa's friend, Jamie, also helped Lisa a great deal and, with the frequent reminders, Lisa began to refer to and use the book. Eventually (about two weeks), Lisa became better organized, and this helped her confidence, which in turn caused her to pay more attention to the teacher because she felt she could do the work required. Lisa still cried from time to time, but overall, the teacher noticed a definite improvement in Lisa's self-esteem and her willingness to try.

Lisa's School Book

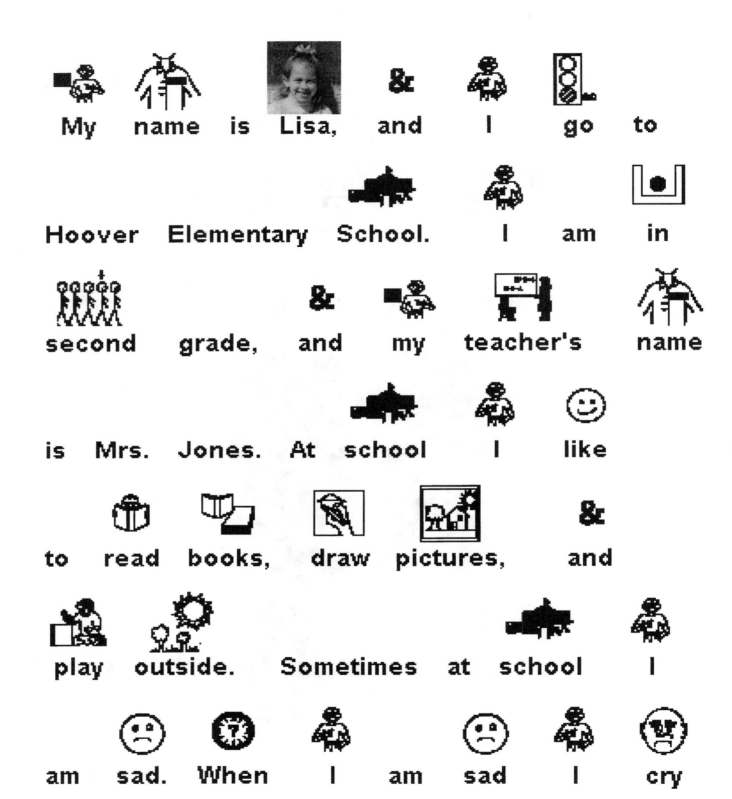

My name is Lisa, and I go to

Hoover Elementary School. I am in

second grade, and my teacher's name

is Mrs. Jones. At school I like

to read books, draw pictures, and

play outside. Sometimes at school I

am sad. When I am sad I cry

and put my head on my desk.

When this happens I can't hear

what the teacher is saying, and then

I can't do my work. I get

sad because I don't have my

materials ready so I can learn and

do my work. To help me with

this,   I   can   keep   only   the   things

I   need   on   my   desk.   I   can

keep   a   pencil,   an   eraser,   and   my

paper   out   on   my   desk.   I   can

listen   to   the   teacher,   and   when   I

don't   understand   something,   I   can

ask   the   teacher   or   ask   my   friend,

aha! Process, Inc. • (800) 424-9484

Jamie, to help me. This way I will not cry, and I can get my work done, and I can be happy.

The next scenario is about a boy named Akeem. He is in a full-day preschool program. Akeem is 4 years old and was taken from his birth mother at 14 months because of abuse and neglect. He has been shuffled around in the foster-care system for almost three years. Akeem is very delayed in his speech and physical abilities. He functions on about a 2-year-old level and is difficult to manage at school and home. At school Akeem is in a developmental classroom where the children have a lot of choice and freedom. Akeem enjoys this, but he has difficulty controlling himself. When the teacher does need for him to comply, he often refuses to do so and runs around the room and tells her no and throws tantrums. Akeem loves to be read to, and his teacher had designed a simple social book for him to read at school to help him follow the classroom rules.

T: Akeem, I have a story to share with you. It's all about you and your day at school. Do you want to hear it?

A: Yep.

T: Why don't you sit in my lap, and we can hold the book together and read it. Look at the cover. Who's that a picture of?

A: Akeem.

T: That's right, that is a picture of Akeem. Now let's read Akeem's book. "My name is Akeem. I go to East Preschool, and my teacher is Mrs. Green. At school I like to paint, play, and run. Sometimes at school I forget the rules, and I tell my teacher no and run away from her. This makes my teacher sad, and it makes me sad, too, because I have to go to time-out. Sometimes I cry and kick and scream. So this won't happen I can remember to sit on my spot on the floor, listen to the teacher, and be good at school. This will make me happy." Do you think you can read this book with me now, Akeem?

A: Yep, let me read.

T: Let's do it together. My name is ...

A: Akeem.

T: I go to ...

A: East Preschool,

T: and my teacher is ...

A: Mrs. Green.

T: At school, I like to ...

A: (pointing at pictures) paint, play, run.

aha! Process, Inc. • (800) 424-9484

T: Sometimes at school I forget the rules, and I tell my teacher ...

A: no and run

T: away from her. This makes my teacher ...

A: sad,

T: and it makes ...

A: Akeem sad, too,

T: because I have to go to ...

A: time-out.

T: Sometimes I ...

A: cry, kick, scream.

T: So this won't happen I can remember to ...

A: (pointing at pictures) sit on my spot, listen to teacher, and be good.

T: This will make Akeem ...

A: happy.

The teacher went on to have Akeem read the story himself, and he did so solely by naming the pictures since he was not developmentally ready to read. Since Akeem was so delayed, the teacher had to refer him often to his social book. Akeem did respond well to the pictures and was able to share his book with classmates and the teacher. It took about three weeks to link the pictures in the book with actual specified behaviors, but Akeem did begin to improve his behavior. After about six weeks of frequent reference to the book, Akeem began to use it independently when he felt he needed a reminder of an appropriate behavior. The teacher continued to use time-outs with Akeem when he broke the rules, and this seemed to work fairly well for short periods of time. Akeem's behavior did improve throughout the course of the school year; the social book was a major contributor to this improvement.

Akeem's School Book

aha! Process, Inc. • (800) 424-9484

My name is Akeem, and I go to East

Preschool, and my teacher is Mrs. Green.

At school I like to paint, play, and run.

Sometimes at school I forget the rules, and I

tell my teacher no and run away from her.

This makes my teacher sad, and it makes me

sad, too, because I have to go to time-out.

Sometimes I cry and kick and scream. So

aha! Process, Inc. • (800) 424-9484

this won't happen I can remember to sit on

my spot on the floor, listen to the teacher,

and be good at school. This will make me

happy.

SUMMARY

This chapter has taken an in-depth look at the use and application of social books and stories. This strategy has proven to be very effective both in the home and school setting. The strategy works well for young children experiencing difficulties related to behavioral and academic problems. The social book and story can take many forms; this technique is not restricted to the four examples shown in this chapter. The reader is encouraged to experiment with this strategy and have some fun with designing and implementing social books and stories for your child or the children with whom you work.

CONCLUSION

A Picture Is *Worth A Thousand Words* has explored the many uses of pictures with young children to make abstract concepts tangible and real. It's of vital importance that adults working with young children – whether in the home environment, school environment, or day-care setting – understand the importance of teaching and communicating on a concrete level with children. Our traditional way of dealing with young children through inappropriate expectations, lack of knowledge of child development and early-learning theories, and simply not meeting their needs has run its course. The children of today are different due to many factors, and they need learning experiences that appropriately connect with their developmental, academic, emotional, and physical needs.

Using pictures with young children to make abstract concepts concrete is a strategy that is only starting to be explored by mainstream educators; this book is not written to be a full-blown research analysis, but rather to suggest practical strategies to educators and parents who are ready to make a difference in the lives of the children they love. Young children do benefit – academically, socially, emotionally, and behaviorally – from being exposed to pictorial representations of abstract concepts.

In closing, many early-childhood educators have known for years how to appropriately meet the needs of young children. Unfortunately, somewhere in the shuffle many of our societal and educational systems have been depriving young children of the important, developmentally rich classroom environments needed to nurture the skills so essential to future learning and social success in school and life. It's only now that we're beginning to see the importance of dealing with young children in ways that more effectively meet their needs. The strategies discussed in this book are a start to communicating and dealing with young children in ways that meet their needs on a concrete level, while simultaneously teaching them abstract concepts. Enjoy the process of using pictures with young children!

aha! Process, Inc. • (800) 424-9484

APPENDIX

Software Resources:

Mayer-Johnson Company, Nonspeech Communication Products.
<u>Boardmaker</u> computer software
P.O. Box 1579
Solana Beach, CA 92075
(619) 550-0084
Fax: (619) 550-0449
E-mail: mayerj@aol.com

Slater Software
<u>Picture It</u> software
351 Badger Lane
Guffey, CO 80820
(719) 479-2255
Fax: (719) 479-2254

Additional Reading:

Albrecht, K., & Plantz, M. (Eds.). (1991). <u>Developmentally Appropriate Practice in School-Age Child Care Programs</u>. Alexandria, VA: Project Home Safe.

Allen, E., & Marotz, L. (1989). <u>Developmental Profiles – Birth to Six</u>. Albany, NY: Delmar Publishers.

American Association of School Administrators. (1992). <u>Getting Your Child Ready for School … and the School Ready for Your Child</u>. Arlington, VA: Author.

American Association of School Administrators. (1992). <u>The Nongraded Primary: Making Schools Fit Children</u>. Arlington, VA: Author.

Association for Childhood Education International. (April 1987). The child-centered kindergarten. <u>Childhood Education</u>, 63:235-242.

Barth, P., & Mitchell, R. (1992). <u>Smart Start: Elementary Education for the 21st Century</u>. Golden, CO: North American Press.

Beaty, J. (1992). <u>Preschool Appropriated Practices</u>. Orlando, FL: Holt, Rinehart, and Winston.

Boyer, E.L. (1986). <u>The Early Years and the Nation's Future</u>. Washington, DC: National Press Club.

Boyer, E.L. (1991). <u>Ready to Learn: A Mandate for the Nation</u>. The Carnegie Foundation for the Advancement of Teaching. Princeton, NJ: Princeton University Press.

Bredekamp, S. (1997). <u>Developmentally Appropriate Practice in Early Childhood Programs (revised edition)</u>. Washington, DC: National Association for the Education of Young Children.

Bredekamp, S., & Rosengrant, T. (Eds.). (1992). <u>Reaching Potentials: Appropriate Curriculum and Assessment for Young Children – Vol. 1</u>. Washington, DC: National Association for the Education of Young Children.

Bredekamp, S., & Shepard, L.A. (1989). How to best protect children from inappropriate school expectations, practices, and policies. <u>Young Children</u>, 44:14-24.

Caine, R.N., & Caine, G. (1994). <u>Making Connections: Teaching and the Human Brain</u>. New York, NY: Addison-Wesley.

Caine, R.N., Caine, G., & Crowell, S. (1994). <u>Mindshifts: A Brain-Based Process for Restructuring Schools and Renewing Education</u>. Tucson, AZ: Zephyr Press.

Carnegie Corporation of New York. (1994). <u>Starting Points: Meeting the Needs of Our Youngest Children</u>. New York, NY: Carnegie Corp.

Charlesworth, R. (1989). Behind before they start? Deciding how to deal with the risk of kindergarten failure. <u>Young Children</u>, 44:5-13.

Colletta, A. (1991). <u>What's Best for Kids</u>. Rosemont, NJ: Modern Learning Press.

Cornell, D.R. (1987). The first 30 years were the fairest: Notes from the kindergarten and ungraded primary (K-1-2). <u>Young Children</u>, 48:30-39.

Davis, M.D. (April 1989). Preparing teachers for developmentally appropriate kindergarten classrooms. <u>Dimensions</u>, 4-7.

Elkind, D. (1987). <u>Miseducation: Preschoolers at Risk</u>. New York, NY: Alfred A. Knopf.

Elkind, D. (October 1989). Developmentally appropriate practice: Philosophical and practical implications. <u>Phi Delta Kappan</u>, 113-117.

Elkind, D. (1998). <u>Reinventing Childhood: Raising and educating children in a changing world</u>. Rosemont, NJ: Modern Learning Press.

Epstein, P. (May 1990). Are public schools ready for Montessori? <u>Principal</u>, 20-22.

Faber, A., & Mazlish, E. (1980). <u>How to Talk So Kids Will Listen and Listen So Kids Will Talk</u>. New York, NY: Avon Books.

George, P. (1992). <u>How to Untrack Your School</u>. Alexandria, VA: Association for Supervision and Curriculum Development.

Goodlad, J., & Anderson, R.H. (1987). <u>The Nongraded Elementary School (revised edition)</u>. New York, NY: Teachers College Press.

Grant, J. (1998). <u>Developmental Education in an Era of High Standards</u>. Rosemont, NJ: Modern Learning Press.

Healey, J. (1998). <u>Failure To Connect</u>. New York, NY: Simon & Schuster.

Hohmann, M., & Weikart, D. (1995). <u>Educating Young Children</u>. Ypsilanti, MI: High/Scope Press.

Holloman, S. (1990). Retention and redshirting: The dark side of kindergarten. <u>Principal</u>, 69:13-15.

National Association of Elementary School Principals. (1990). <u>Early Childhood Education and the Elementary School Principal: Standards for Quality Programs for Young Children</u>. Alexandria, VA: National Association of Elementary School Principals.

Peck, J., McCaig, G., & Sapp, M. (1988). <u>Kindergarten Policies: What is Best for Children?</u> Washington, DC: National Association for the Education of Young Children.

Schickendanz, J. (1986). <u>More Than ABC's: The Early Stages of Reading and Writing</u>. Washington, DC: National Association for the Education of Young Children.

Schultz, T. (October 1989). Testing and retentions of young children: Moving from controversy to reform. <u>Phi Delta Kappan</u>, 125-129.

Schweinhart, L.J. (May 1988). How important is child-initiated activity? <u>Principal</u>, 6-10.

Schweinhart, L.J. (1998). Why curriculum matters in early childhood programs. <u>Educational Leadership</u>, 55:57-60.

Seebaum, M. (Winter/Spring 1995). Taking the first steps in implementing a multiage program. <u>Society for Developmental Education News</u>, 3-7.

Society for Developmental Education. (1993). <u>Multiage Classrooms: The Ungrading of America's Schools</u>. Peterborough, NH: Author.

aha! Process, Inc. • (800) 424-9484

Strickland, D., & Morrow, L. (Eds.). (1989). <u>Emerging Literacy: Young Children Learn to Read and Write</u>. Newark, DE: International Reading Association.

Sylwester, R. (1995). <u>A Celebration of Neurons: An Educator's Guide to the Human Brain</u>. Alexandria, VA: Association for Supervision and Curriculum Development.

Wood, C. (1997). <u>Yardsticks</u>. Greenfield, MA: Northeast Foundation for Children, Inc.

BIBLIOGRAPHY

Armstrong, T. (1987). <u>In Their Own Way: Discovering and Encouraging Your Child's Personal Learning Style</u>. New York, NY: Putnam.

Birren, F. (1978a). <u>Color and Human Response</u>. New York, NY: Van Nostrand Reinhold.

Birren, F. (1978b). <u>Color in Your World</u>. New York, NY: Collier.

Bredekamp, S. (1997). <u>Developmentally Appropriate Practice in Early Childhood Programs, Revised Edition</u>. Washington, DC: National Association for the Education of Young Children.

Copple, C., Sigel, I.E., & Sounders, P. (1984). <u>Educating the Young Thinker: Classroom strategies for cognitive growth</u>. Hillsdale, NJ: Erlbaum.

Dewey, J. (1933). <u>How We Think: A Restatement of the Relation of Reflective Thinking to the Educative Process</u>. Boston, MA: Heath.

Edwards, C., Gandini, L., Forman, G. (Eds.). (1993). <u>The Hundred Languages of Children: The Reggio Emelia approach to early childhood education</u>. Norwood, NJ: Ablex.

Edwards, C., & Springate K. (1995). Encouraging creativity in early childhood classrooms. Urbana, IL: Educational Resources Information Consortium (ERIC) Clearinghouse on Elementary and Early Childhood Education.

Evans, B. (1996). Helping children resolve disputes and conflicts. In <u>Supporting Young Learners 2</u>, 27-34. Brickman, N. (Ed.). Ypsilanti, MI: High/Scope Press.

Forman, G. (1994). Different media, different languages. In <u>Reflections on the Reggio Emelia Approach</u>, 37-46. Katz, L., & Cesarone, B. (Eds.). Urbana, IL: Educational Resources Information Consortium (ERIC) Clearinghouse on Elementary and Early Childhood Education.

Hohmann, M., & Weikart, D. (1995). <u>Educating Young Children</u>. Ypsilanti, MI: High/Scope Press.

Howard, P.J. (1994). <u>The Owner's Manual for the Brain: Everyday Applications from Mind-Brain Research</u>. Austin, TX: Bard Press.

Joos, M. (1967). <u>The Styles of the Five Clocks</u>. Language and Cultural Diversity in American Education. 1972. Abrahams, R.D., and Troike, R.C. (Eds.). Englewood Cliffs, NJ: Prentice-Hall, Inc.

Payne, R.K. (1998). <u>A Framework for Understanding Poverty (Revised Edition)</u>. Highlands, TX: RFT Publishing.

Piaget, J. (1952). <u>The Origins of Intelligence in Children</u>. New York, NY: International Universities Press.

Piaget, J. (1973). To Understand is to Invent. New York, NY: Grossman.

Satir, V. (1988). The New Peoplemaking. Mountain View, CA: Science & Behavior Books, Inc.

Wells, G. (1986). The Meaning Makers: Children Learning Language and Using Language to Learn. Portsmouth, NH: Heinemann Educational Books.

ABOUT THE AUTHOR

Matthew S. Seebaum, Ed.D.

Matthew S. "Matt" Seebaum is a distinguished educator with a wide array of experiences, many of which have had a hand in molding his deeply held beliefs about the way young children learn – and have inspired the creation of this book. Of particular interest to the author is the use of pictures to convey concrete meanings to young children, including those with special needs. This practice bridges the gap between the concrete and abstract in the classroom (and other school environments) to enhance both early learning and appropriate social behavior. As a spokesman and advocate for young children, Matt Seebaum sees making a difference in their lives as his life's work.

Seebaum began his career at the University of Wyoming Lab School in a multiage classroom environment, moved to Texas to pursue graduate studies and continue his work as a teacher. He later became an administrator and served as an early childhood specialist and principal of an early childhood school. He currently is an elementary school principal in Colorado. He holds a bachelor's degree from the University of Wyoming, Laramie; a master's degree from Texas Tech University, Lubbock; and a doctorate from Nova Southeastern University, Fort Lauderdale, Florida.

In his spare time, Dr. Seebaum enjoys writing, and he travels often to conduct workshops at conventions, as well as for schools and school districts. Living in Colorado allows him to enjoy the mountains and the great outdoors. He has a particular interest in urban education and devotes much of his time to working with disadvantaged children and families. In addition, he and his wife have two young children of their own who keep them very busy and happy.

aha! Process, Inc.
PO Box 727, Highlands, TX 77562-0727
(800) 424-9484; fax (281) 426-5600

www.ahaprocess.com

For more information about the availability of scheduling Dr. Seebaum to present the workshop, A Picture Is Worth A Thousand Words, please contact our office.

ORDER FORM

Please send me:

_____ Copy/copies of *A Picture IS Worth A Thousand Words*

Books: 1-4 books $18/each+$4.50 first book plus $2.00 each additional book for shipping/handling

     5 or more $15/each + 8% shipping/handling

Subtotal: $ _____
Shipping: $ _____
Sales tax: $ _____ (7.75% in Texas)
Total: $_____

UPS SHIP TO ADDRESS (no post office boxes, please):

Name: _____
Organization: _____
Address: _____
_____
Phone: _____ Email: _____

Method of Payment:
PO # _____
Credit card type: _____ Exp: _____
Credit card number: _____
Check: $ _____ Check # _____

Thanks for your order!

Check the website for our most current offerings!   **www.ahaprocess.com**